# THE GITA
## FOR THE YOUTH

A Compilation
from the Writings of Sri Aurobindo

Sri Aurobindo Society
# AUROPUBLICATIONS
POWERFUL THOUGHTS, INSPIRING VISION

First Edition: 1989
Second Edition: 2022

Price Rs. 95
ISBN 978-81-7060-039-8

**Published by**
AuroPublications, Sri Aurobindo Society, Puducherry
Website: www.auropublications.org | www.aurosociety.org
Email: info@auropublications.org

© Sri Aurobindo Ashram Trust 1989
Compiled by Guru Pershad
Writings of Sri Aurobindo are copyright
Sri Aurobindo Ashram Trust, Puducherry

Printed at Sudarshan Graphics, Chennai, India

# CONTENTS

# Introduction

*This book has been compiled entirely from Sri Aurobindo's* Essays on the Gita. *The compilation has been dione by a sadhak who is a disciple of Sri Aurobindo and the Mother. In 1972, he had mentioned to the Mother his aspiration to bring out a small book on the Gita, of about 100 pages, specially suited to the young. The Mother had approved and blessed the project. However, due to various reasons, the compiler could take up the work only in 1987. Now that it is completed, he gratefully offers it at the feet of the Master and the Mother.*

*The Gita has a message for all. In this compilation, the stress has been on those passages which could inspire the Youth and guide and help them towards a new future. If this book can lead even a few of its readers to go to the complete work of Sri Aurobindo and to practise and live the Yoga of the Gita, it would have served its purpose.*

*The titles and subtitles by the compiler and are based on Sri Aurobindo's blessings.*

# Our Demand and Need from the Gita

The world abounds with Scriptures sacred and profane, with revelations and half-revelations, with religions and philosophies, sects and schools and systems. To these the many minds of a half-ripe knowledge or no knowledge at all attach themselves with exclusiveness and passion and will have it that this or the other book is alone the eternal Word of God and all others are either impostures or at best imperfectly inspired, that this or that philosophy is the last word of the reasoning intellect and other systems are either errors or saved only by such partial truth in them as links them to the one true philosophical cult. Even the discoveries of physical Science have been elevated into a creed, and in its name religion and spirituality banned as ignorance and superstition, philosophy as frippery and moonshine. And to these bigoted exclusions and vain wranglings even the wise have often lent themselves, misled by some spirit of darkness that has mingled with their light and overshadowed it with some cloud of intellectual egoism or spiritual pride. Mankind seems now indeed inclined to grow a little modester and wiser; we no longer slay our fellows in the name of God's truth or because they have minds differently trained or differently constituted from ours; we are less ready to curse and revile our neighbour because he is wicked or presumptuous enough to differ from us in opinion; we are ready even to admit that Truth is everywhere and cannot be our sole monopoly; we are beginning to look at other religions and philosophies for the truth and help they contain and no longer

1

merely in order to damn them as false or criticise what we conceive to be their errors. But we are still apt to declare that our truth gives us *the* supreme knowledge which other religions or philosophies have missed or only imperfectly grasped so that they deal either with subsidiary and inferior aspects of the truth of things, or can merely prepare less evolved minds for the heights to which we have arrived. And we are still prone to force upon ourselves or others the whole sacred mass of the book or gospel we admire, insisting that all shall be accepted as eternally valid truth and no iota or underline or diaeresis denied its part of the plenary inspiration.

## How to Approach the Gita

It may therefore be useful in approaching an ancient Scripture, such as the Veda, Upanishads or Gita, to indicate precisely the spirit in which we approach it and what exactly we think we may derive from it that is of value to humanity and its future. First of all, there is undoubtedly a Truth one and eternal which we are seeking, from which all other truth derives, by the light of which all other truth finds its right place, explanation and relation to the scheme of knowledge. But precisely for that reason it cannot be shut up in a single trenchant formula, it is not likely to be found in its entirety or in all its bearings in any single philosophy or scripture or uttered altogether and for ever by any one teacher, thinker, prophet or Avatar. Nor has it been wholly found by us if our view of it necessitates the intolerant exclusion of the truth underlying other systems; for when we reject passionately, we mean simply that we cannot appreciate and explain. Second, this Truth, though it is one and eternal, expresses itself in Time and through the mind of man; therefore every Scripture must necessarily contain two elements, one temporary, perishable, belonging to the ideas of the period and country in which it was produced, the other eternal and imperishable and applicable in all ages and countries. Moreover, in the statement of the Truth the actual form given to it, the system and arrangement, the metaphysical and intellectual mould, the precise expression used must be largely subject to the mutations of Time and cease to have the same force; for the human intellect modifies itself always; continually dividing and putting together it is obliged to shift its divisions continually and to rearrange its syntheses; it is always leaving old expression and symbol for new or, if it uses the old, it so changes its connotation or at least its exact content and association that we can never be quite sure of understanding an ancient book of this kind precisely in the sense and spirit it bore to its contemporaries. What is of entirely permanent value is that which besides being universal has been experienced, lived and seen with a higher vision than the intellectual vision.

*

But what we can do with profit is to seek in the Gita for the actual living truths it contains, apart from their metaphysical form, to extract from it what can help us or the world at large, and to put it in the most natural and vital form and expression we can find that will be suitable to the mentality and helpful to the spiritual needs of our present-day humanity. No doubt in this attempt we may mix a good deal of error born of our own individuality and of the ideas in which we live, as did greater men before us, but if we steep ourselves in the spirit of this great Scripture and, above all, if we have tried to live in that spirit, we may be sure of finding in it as much real truth as we are capable of receiving as well as the spiritual influence and actual help that, personally, we were intended to derive from it. And that is after all what Scriptures were written to give; the rest is academical disputation or theological dogma. Only those Scriptures, religions, philosophies which can be thus constantly renewed, relived, their stuff of permanent truth constantly reshaped and developed in the inner thought and spiritual experience of a developing humanity, continue to be of living importance to mankind. The rest remain as monuments of the past, but have no actual force or vital impulse for the future.

## The Synthetic Spirit of the Gita

In the Gita there is very little that is merely local or temporal and its spirit is so large, profound and universal that even this little can easily be universalised without the sense of the teaching suffering any diminution or violation; rather by giving an ampler scope to it than belonged to the country and epoch, the teaching gains in depth, truth and power. Often indeed the Gita itself suggests the wider scope that can in this way be given to an idea in itself local or limited.

*

The philosophical system of the Gita, its arrangement of truth, is not that part of its teaching which is the most vital, profound, eternally durable; but most of the material of which the system is composed, the principal ideas suggestive and penetrating which are woven into its complex harmony, are eternally valuable and valid; for they are not merely the luminous ideas or striking speculations of a philosophic intellect, but rather enduring truths of spiritual experience, verifiable facts of our highest psychological possibilities which no attempt to read deeply the mystery of existence can afford to neglect.

*

The language of the Gita, the structure of thought, the combination and balancing of ideas belong neither to the temper of a sectarian teacher nor to the spirit of a rigorous analytical dialectics cutting off one angle of the truth to exclude all the others; but rather there is a wide, undulating, encircling movement of ideas which is the manifestation of a vast synthetic mind and a rich synthetic experience. This is one of those great syntheses in which Indian spirituality has been as rich as in its creation of the more intensive, exclusive movements of knowledge and religious realisation that follow out with an absolute concentration one clue, one path to its extreme issues. It does not cleave asunder, but reconciles and unifies.

*

Our object, then, in studying the Gita will not be a scholastic or academical scrutiny of its thought, nor to place its philosophy in the history of metaphysical speculation, nor shall we deal with it in the manner of the analytical dialectician. We approach it for help and light, and our aim must be to distinguish its essential and living message, that in it on which humanity has to seize for its perfection and its highest spiritual welfare.

# THE DIVINE TEACHER

## A Unique Feature

The peculiarity of the Gita among the great religious books of the world is that it does not stand apart as a work by itself, the fruit of the spiritual life of a creative personality like Christ, Mahomed or Buddha or of an epoch of pure spiritual searching like the Veda and Upanishads, but is given as an episode in an epic history of nations and their wars and men and their deeds and arises out of a critical moment in the soul of one of its leading personages face-to-face with the crowning action of his life, a work terrible, violent and sanguinary, at the point when he must either recoil from it altogether or carry it through to its inexorable completion.... It matters little whether or not, as modern criticism supposes, the Gita is a later composition inserted into the mass of the Mahabharata by its author in order to invest its teaching with the authority and popularity of the great national epic. There seem to me to be strong grounds against this supposition for which, besides, the evidence, extrinsic or internal, is in the last degree scanty and insufficient. But even if it be sound, there remains the fact that the author has not only taken pains to interweave his work inextricably into the vast web of the larger poem, but is careful again and again to remind us of the situation from which the teaching has arisen; he returns to it prominently, not only at the end, but in the middle of his profoundest philosophical disquisitions. We must accept the insistence of the author, and give its full importance to this recurrent preoccupation of the Teacher and the disciple. The teaching of the Gita must therefore be regarded not merely in the light of a general spiritual philosophy or ethical doctrine, but as bearing upon a practical crisis in the application of ethics and spirituality to human life. For what that crisis stands, what is the significance of the battle of Kurukshetra and its effect on Arjuna's inner being, we have first to determine if we would grasp the central drift of the ideas of the Gita.

*

There are indeed three things in the Gita which are spiritually significant, almost symbolic, typical of the profoundest relations and problems of the spiritual life and of human existence at its roots; they are the divine personality of the Teacher, his characteristic relations with his disciple and the occasion of his teaching. The teacher is God himself descended into humanity; the disciple is the first, as we might say in modern language, the representative man of his age, closest friend and chosen instrument of the Avatar, his protagonist in an immense work and struggle the secret purpose of which is unknown to the actors in it, known only to the incarnate Godhead who guides it all from behind the veil of his unfathomable mind of knowledge; the occasion is the violent crisis of that work and struggle at the moment when the anguish and moral difficulty and blind violence of its apparent movements forces itself with the shock of a visible revelation on the mind of its representative man and raises the whole question of the meaning of God in the world and the goal and drift and sense of human life and conduct.

## Krishna – the Divine Avatar

India has from ancient times held strongly a belief in the reality of the Avatara, the descent into form, the revelation of the Godhead in humanity..... When the divine Consciousness and Power, taking upon itself the human form and the human mode of action, possesses it not only by powers and magnitudes, by degrees and outward faces of itself but out of its eternal self-knowledge, when the Unborn knows itself and acts in the frame of the mental being and the appearance of birth, that is the height of the conditioned manifestation; it is the full and conscious descent of the Godhead, it is the Avatara.

*

The Gita accepts the human Avatarhood; for the Lord speaks of the repeated, the constant[1] manifestation of the Divine in humanity, when He the eternal Unborn assumes by his Maya, by the power of the infinite Consciousness to clothe itself apparently in finite forms, the conditions of becoming which we call birth. But it is not this upon which stress is laid, but on the transcendent, the cosmic and the internal Divine; it is on the Source of all things and the Master of all and on the Godhead secret in man.

*

## Krishna – Divine and Human

There is the typical, almost the symbolic significance of the human Krishna who stands behind the great action of the Mahabharata, not as its hero, but as its secret centre and

---

[1]*bahūni me vyatītāni janmāni . . . sambhavāmi yuge yuge.*

hidden guide. That action is the action of a whole world of men and nations, some of whom have come as helpers of an effort and result by which they do not personally profit, and to these he is a leader, some as its opponents and to them he also is an opponent, the baffler of their designs and their slayer and he seems even to some of them an instigator of all evil and destroyer of their old order and familiar world and secure conventions of virtue and good; some are representatives of that which has to be fulfilled and to them he is counsellor, helper, friend. Where the action pursues its natural course or the doers of the work have to suffer at the hands of its enemies and undergo the ordeals which prepare them for mastery, the Avatar is unseen or appears only for occasional comfort and aid, but at every crisis his hand is felt, yet in such a way that all imagine themselves to be the protagonists and even Arjuna, his nearest friend and chief instrument, does not perceive that he is an instrument and has to confess at last that all the while he did not really know his divine Friend.

*

Thus the figure of Krishna becomes, as it were, the symbol of the divine dealings with humanity. Through our egoism and ignorance we are moved, thinking that we are the doers of the work, vaunting of ourselves as the real causes of the result, and that which moves us we see only occasionally as some vague or even some human and earthly fountain of knowledge, aspiration, force, some Principle or Light or Power which we acknowledge and adore without knowing what it is until the occasion arises that forces us to stand arrested before the Veil. And the action in which this divine figure moves is the whole wide action of man in life, not merely the inner life, but all this obscure course of  the world which we can judge only by the twilight of the human reason as it opens up dimly before our uncertain advance the little span in front. This is the distinguishing feature of the Gita that it is the culmination of such an action which gives rise to its teaching and assigns that prominence and bold relief to the gospel of works which it enunciates with an emphasis and force we do not find in other Indian Scriptures.

*

Arjuna and Krishna, this human and this divine, stand together not as seers in the peaceful hermitage of meditation, but as fighter and holder of the reins in the clamorous field, in the midst of the hurtling shafts, in the chariot of battle. The Teacher of the Gita is therefore not only the God in man who unveils himself in the word of knowledge, but the God in man who moves our whole world of action, by and for whom all our humanity exists and struggles and labours, towards whom all human life travels and progresses. He is the secret Master of works and sacrifice and the Friend of the human peoples.

# THE HUMAN DISCIPLE

Arjuna, as we have seen, is the representative man of a great world-struggle and divinely- guided movement of men and nations; in the Gita he typifies the human soul of action brought face-to-face through that action in its highest and most violent crisis with the problem of human life and its apparent incompatibility with the spiritual state or even with a purely ethical ideal of perfection.

...Arjuna is the man of action and not of knowledge, the fighter, never the seer or the thinker.

From the beginning of the Gita this characteristic temperament of the disciple is clearly indicated and it is maintained throughout. It becomes first evident in the manner in which he is awakened to the sense of what he is doing, the great psychological motives which make him recoil from the whole terrible catastrophe. They are not the thoughts, the standpoint, the motives of a philosophical or even of a deeply reflective mind, or a spiritual temperament confronted with the same or a similar problem. They are those, as we might say, of the practical or the pragmatic man, the emotional, sensational, moral and intelligent human being not habituated to profound and original reflection or any sounding of the depths, accustomed rather to high but fixed standards of thought and action and a confident treading through all vicissitudes and difficulties, who now finds all his standards failing him and all the basis of his confidence in himself and his life shorn away from under him at a single stroke. That is the nature of the crisis which he undergoes.

## The Crisis of Arjuna

It is typical again of the pragmatic man that it is through his sensations that he awakens to the meaning of his action. He has asked his friend and charioteer to place him between the two armies, not with any profounder idea, but with the proud intention of viewing and looking in the face of these myriads of the champions of unrighteousness whom he has to meet and conquer and slay "in this holiday of fight" so that right may prevail. It is as he gazes that the revelation of the meaning of a civil and domestic war comes home to him, a war in which not only men of the same race, the same nation, the same clan, but those of the same family and household stand on opposite sides. All whom the social man holds most dear and sacred, he must meet as enemies and slay, – the worshipped teacher and preceptor, the old friend, comrade and companion in arms, grandsires, uncles, those who were related to him as father, son, grandson, connections by blood and connections by marriage, – all these social ties have to be cut asunder by the sword. It is not that he did not know these things before, but he has never realised it all; obsessed by his claims and wrongs and by the principles of his life, the struggle for the right, the duty of the Kshatriya to protect justice and the law and fight and beat down injustice and lawless violence, he has neither thought it out deeply nor felt it in his heart and at the core of his life. And now it is shown in his vision by the divine charioteer, placed sensationally before his eyes, and comes home to him like a blow delivered at the very centre of his sensational, vital and emotional being. The first result is a violent sensational and physical crisis which produces a disgust of the action and its material objects and of life itself. He rejects the vital aim pursued by egoistic humanity in its action,—happiness and enjoyment; he rejects the vital aim of the Kshatriya, victory and rule and power and the government of men. What after all is this fight for justice when reduced to its practical terms, but just this, a fight for the interests of himself, his brothers and his party, for possession and enjoyment and rule? But at such a cost these things are not worth having. For they are of no value in themselves, but only as a means to the right maintenance of social and national life, and it is these very aims that in the person of his kin and his race he is about to destroy. And then comes the cry of the emotions. These are they for whose sake life and happiness are desired, our "own people". Who would consent to slay these for the sake of all the earth, or even for the kingdom of the three worlds? What pleasure can there be in life, what happiness, what satisfaction in oneself after such a deed? The whole thing is a dreadful sin,—for now the moral sense awakens to justify the revolt of the sensations and the emotions. It is a sin, there is no right nor justice in mutual slaughter; especially are those who are to be slain the natural objects of reverence and of love, those without whom one would not care to live, and to violate these sacred feelings can be no virtue, can be nothing but a heinous crime. Granted that the offence, the aggression, the first sin, the crimes of greed and selfish passion which have brought things to such a pass came from the other side; yet armed resistance to wrong under such circumstances would be itself a sin and crime worse than theirs because they are blinded by passion and unconscious of guilt, while on this side it would be with a clear sense of guilt that the sin would be committed. And for what?

For the maintenance of family morality, of the social law and the law of the nation? These are the very standards that will be destroyed by this civil war; the family itself will be brought to the point of annihilation, corruption of morals and loss of the purity of race will be engendered, the eternal laws of the race and moral law of the family will be destroyed. Ruin of the race, the collapse of its high traditions, ethical degradation and hell for the authors of such a crime, these are the only practical results possible of this monstrous civil strife. "Therefore," cries Arjuna, casting down the divine bow and inexhaustible quiver given to him by the gods for that tremendous hour, "it is more for my welfare that the sons of Dhritarashtra armed should slay me unarmed and unresisting. I will not fight."

The character of this inner crisis is therefore not the questioning of the thinker; it is not a recoil from the appearances of life and a turning of the eye inward in search of the truth of things, the real meaning of existence and a solution or an escape from the dark riddle of the world. It is the sensational, emotional and moral revolt of the man hitherto satisfied with action and its current standards who finds himself cast by them into a hideous chaos where they are in violent conflict with each other and with themselves and there is no moral standing-ground left, nothing to lay hold of and walk by, no *dharma*. That for the soul of action in the mental being is the worst possible crisis, failure and overthrow. The revolt itself is the most elemental and simple possible; sensationally, the elemental feeling of horror, pity and disgust; vitally, the loss of attraction and faith in the recognised and familiar objects of action and aims of life; emotionally, the recoil of the ordinary feelings of social man, affection, reverence, desire of a common happiness and satisfaction, from a stern duty outraging them all; morally, the elementary sense of sin and hell and rejection of "blood-stained enjoyments"; practically, the sense that the standards of action have led to a result which destroys the practical aims of action. But the whole upshot is that all-embracing inner bankruptcy which Arjuna expresses when he says that his whole conscious being, not the thought alone but heart and vital desires and all, are utterly bewildered and can find nowhere the *dharma*, nowhere any valid law of action. For this alone he takes refuge as a disciple with Krishna; give me, he practically asks, that which I have lost, a true law, a clear rule of action, a path by which I can again confidently walk. He does not ask for the secret of life or of the world, the meaning and purpose of it all, but for a *dharma*.

Yet it is precisely this secret for which he does not ask, or at least so much of the knowledge as is necessary to lead him into a higher life, to which the divine Teacher intends to lead this disciple; for he means him to give up all *dharmas* except the one broad and vast rule of living consciously in the Divine and acting from that consciousness.

*

To such a disciple the Teacher of the Gita gives his divine teaching. He seizes him at a moment of his psychological development by egoistic action when all the mental, moral, emotional values of the ordinary egoistic and social life of man have collapsed in a sudden bankruptcy, and he has to lift him up out of this lower life into a higher consciousness, out of ignorant attachment to action into that which transcends, yet originates and orders action, out of ego into Self, out of life in mind, vitality and body into that higher nature beyond mind which is the status of the Divine. He has at the same time to give him that for which he asks and for which he is inspired to seek by the guidance within him, a new Law of life and action high above the insufficient rule of the ordinary human existence with its endless conflicts and oppositions, perplexities and illusory certainties, a higher Law by which the soul shall be free from this bondage of works and yet powerful to act and conquer in the vast liberty of its divine being. For the action must be performed, the world must fulfil its cycles and the soul of the human being must not turn back in ignorance from the work it is here to do. The whole course of the teaching of the Gita is determined and directed, even in its widest wheelings, towards the fulfilment of these three objects.

# The Core of the Teaching

The Gita with its rich and many-sided thought, its synthetical grasp of different aspects of the spiritual life and the fluent winding motion of its argument lends itself, even more than other scriptures, to one-sided misrepresentations born of a partisan intellectuality…. The Gita lends itself easily to this kind of error, because it is easy, by throwing particular emphasis on one of its aspects or even on some salient and emphatic text and putting all the rest of the eighteen chapters into the background or making them a subordinate and auxiliary teaching, to turn it into a partisan of our own doctrine or dogma.

## A Wrong Interpretation

But today, since in fact the modern mind began to recognise and deal at all with the Gita, the tendency is to subordinate its elements of knowledge and devotion, to take advantage of its continual insistence on action and to find in it a scripture of the Karmayoga, a Light leading us on the path of action, a Gospel of Works. Undoubtedly, the Gita is a Gospel of Works, but of works which culminate in knowledge, that is, in spiritual realisation and quietude, and of works motived by devotion, that is, a conscious surrender of one's whole self first into the hands and then into the being of the Supreme, and not at all of works as they are understood by the modern mind, not at all an action dictated by egoistic and altruistic, by personal, social, humanitarian motives, principles, ideals. Yet this is what present-day interpretations seek to make of the Gita. We are told continually by many authoritative voices that the Gita, opposing in this the ordinary ascetic and quietistic tendency of Indian thought and spirituality, proclaims with no uncertain sound the gospel of human action, the ideal of disinterested performance of social duties, nay, even, it would seem, the quite modern ideal of social service. To all this I can only reply that very patently and even on the very surface of it, the Gita does nothing of the kind and that this is a modern misreading, a reading of the modern mind into an ancient book, of the present-day European or Europeanised intellect into a thoroughly antique, a thoroughly Oriental and Indian teaching. That which the Gita teaches is not a human, but a divine action; not the performance of social duties, but the abandonment of all other standards of duty or conduct for a selfless performance of the divine will working through our nature; not social service, but the action of the Best, the God-possessed, the Master-men done impersonally for the sake of the world and as a sacrifice to Him who stands behind man and Nature.

In other words, the Gita is not a book of practical ethics, but of the spiritual life. The modern mind is just not the European mind, such as it has become after having abandoned not only the philosophic idealism of the highest Graeco-Roman culture from which it started, but the Christian devotionalism of the Middle Ages; these it has replaced by or transmuted into a practical idealism and social, patriotic and philanthropic devotion. It has got rid of God or kept Him only for Sunday use and erected in His place man as its deity and society as its visible idol. At its best it is practical, ethical, social, pragmatic, altruistic, humanitarian. Now all these things are good, are especially needed at the present day, are part of the divine Will or they would not have become so dominant in humanity. Nor is there any reason why the divine man, the man who lives in the Brahmic consciousness, in the God-being should not be all of these things in his action; he will be, if they are the best ideal of the age, the Yugadharma, and there is no yet higher ideal to be established, no great radical change to be effected. For he is, as the Teacher points out to his disciple, the best who has to set the standard for others; and in fact Arjuna is called upon to live according to the highest ideals of his age and the prevailing culture, but with knowledge, with understanding of that which lay behind, and not as ordinary men, with a following of the merely outward law and rule.

But the point here is that the modern mind has exiled from its practical motive-power the two essential things, God or the Eternal and spirituality or the God-state, which are the master conceptions of the Gita. It lives in humanity only, and the Gita would have us live in God, though for the world in God; in its life, heart and intellect only, and the Gita would have us live in the spirit; in the mutable Being who is "all creatures", and the Gita would have us live also in the Immutable and the Supreme; in the changing march of Time, and the Gita would have us live in the Eternal. Or if these higher things are now beginning to be vaguely envisaged, it is only to make them subservient to man and society; but God and spirituality exist in their own right and not as adjuncts. And in practice the lower in us must learn to exist for the higher, in order that the higher also may in us consciously exist for the lower, to draw it nearer to its own altitudes.

## Gita and the Meaning of Duty

Therefore it is a mistake to interpret the Gita from the standpoint of the mentality of today and force it to teach us the disinterested performance of duty as the highest and all-sufficient law. A little consideration of the situation with which the Gita deals will show us that this could not be its meaning. For the whole point of the teaching, that from which it arises, that which compels the disciple to seek the Teacher, is an inextricable clash of the various related conceptions of duty ending in the collapse of the whole useful intellectual and moral edifice erected by the human mind. In human life some sort of a clash arises fairly often, as for instance between domestic duties and the call of the country or the cause, or between the claim of the country and the good of humanity or some larger religious or moral principle. An inner situation may even arise, as with the Buddha, in which all duties have to be abandoned, trampled on, flung aside in order to follow the call of the Divine within. I cannot think that the Gita would solve such an inner situation by sending Buddha back to his wife and father and the government of the Sakya State, or would direct a Ramakrishna to become a Pundit in a vernacular school and disinterestedly teach little boys their lessons, or bind down a Vivekananda to support his family and for that to follow dispassionately the law or medicine or journalism. The Gita does not teach the disinterested performance of duties but the following of the divine life, the abandonment of all dharmas, *sarvadharmān*, to take refuge in the Supreme alone, and the divine activity of a Buddha, a Ramakrishna, a Vivekananda is perfectly in consonance with this teaching.

Nay, although the Gita prefers action to inaction, it does not rule out the renunciation of works, but accepts it as one of the ways to the Divine. If that can only be attained by renouncing works and life and all duties and the call is strong within us, then into the bonfire they must go, and there is no help for it. The call of God is imperative and cannot be weighed against any other considerations.

But here there is this farther difficulty that the action which Arjuna must do is one from which his moral sense recoils. It is his duty to fight, you say? But that duty has now become to his mind a terrible sin. How does it help him or solve his difficulty, to tell him that he must do his duty disinterestedly, dispassionately? He will want to know which is his duty or how it can be his duty to destroy in a sanguinary massacre his kin, his race and his country. He is told that he has right on his side, but that does not and cannot satisfy him, because his very point is that the justice of his legal claim does not justify him in supporting it by a pitiless massacre destructive to the future of his nation. Is he then to act dispassionately in the sense of not caring whether it is a sin or what its consequences may be so long as he does his duty as a soldier? That may be the teaching of a State, of politicians, of lawyers, of ethical casuists; it can never be the teaching of a great religious and philosophical Scripture which sets out to solve the problem of life and action from the very roots. And if that is what the Gita has to say on a most poignant moral and spiritual problem, we must put it out of the list of the world's Scriptures and thrust it, if anywhere, then into our library of political science and ethical casuistry.

Undoubtedly, the Gita does, like the Upanishads, teach the equality which rises above sin and virtue, beyond good and evil, but only as a part of the Brahmic consciousness and for the man who is on the path and advanced enough to fulfil the supreme rule. It does not preach indifference to good and evil for the ordinary life of man, where such a doctrine would have the most pernicious consequences. On the contrary it affirms that the doers of evil shall not attain God. Therefore if Arjuna simply seeks to fulfil in the best way the ordinary law of man's life, disinterested performance of what he feels to be a sin, a thing of Hell, will not help him, even though that sin be his duty as a soldier. He must refrain from what his conscience abhors though a thousand duties were shattered to pieces.

We must remember that duty is an idea which in practice rests upon social conceptions. We may extend the term beyond its proper connotation and talk of our duty to ourselves or we may, if we like, say in a transcendent sense that it was Buddha's duty to abandon all, or even that it is the ascetic's duty to sit motionless in a cave! But this is obviously to play with words. Duty is a relative term and depends upon our relation to others. It is a father's duty, as a father, to nurture and educate his children; a lawyer's to do his best for his client even if he knows him to be guilty and his defence to be a lie; a soldier's to fight and shoot to order even if he kill his own kin and countrymen; a judge's to send the guilty to prison and hang the murderer. And so long as these positions are accepted, the duty remains clear, a practical matter of course even when it is not a point of honour or affection, and overrides the absolute religious or moral law. But what if the inner view is changed, if the lawyer is awakened to the absolute sinfulness of falsehood, the judge becomes convinced that capital punishment is a crime against humanity, the man called upon to the battlefield feels, like the conscientious objector of today or as a Tolstoy would feel, that in no circumstances is it permissible to take human life any more than to eat human flesh? It is obvious that here the moral law which is above all relative duties must prevail; and that law depends on no social relation or conception of duty but on the awakened inner perception of man, the moral being.

There are in the world, in fact, two different laws of conduct each valid on its own plane, the rule principally dependent on external status and the rule independent of status and entirely dependent on the thought and conscience. The Gita does not teach us to subordinate the higher plane to the lower, it does not ask the awakened moral consciousness to slay itself on the altar of duty as a sacrifice and victim to the law of the social status. It calls us higher and not lower; from the conflict of the two planes it bids us ascend to a supreme poise above the mainly practical, above the purely ethical, to the Brahmic consciousness. It replaces the conception of social duty by a divine obligation. The subjection to external law gives place to a certain principle of inner self-determination of action proceeding by the soul's freedom from the tangled law of works. And this, as we shall see,—the Brahmic consciousness, the soul's freedom from works and the determination of works in the nature by the Lord within and above us,— is the kernel of the Gita's teaching with regard to action.

## The Work to be Done

The Gita can only be understood, like any other great work of the kind, by studying it in its entirety and as a developing argument. But the modern interpreters, starting from the great writer Bankim Chandra Chatterji who first gave to the Gita this new sense of a Gospel of Duty, have laid an almost exclusive stress on the first three or four chapters and in those on the idea of equality, on the expression *kartavyam karma*, the work that is to be done, which they render by duty, and on the phrase "Thou hast a right to action, but none to the fruits of action" which is now popularly quoted as the great word, *mahāvākya*, of the Gita. The rest of the eighteen chapters with their high philosophy are given a secondary importance, except indeed the great vision in the eleventh. This is natural enough for the modern mind which is, or has been till yesterday, inclined to be impatient of metaphysical subtleties and far-off spiritual seekings, eager to get to work and, like Arjuna himself, mainly concerned for a workable law of works, a *dharma*. But it is the wrong way to handle this Scripture.

The equality which the Gita preaches is not disinterestedness,—the great command to Arjuna given *after* the foundation and main structure of the teaching have been laid and built, "Arise, slay thy enemies, enjoy a prosperous kingdom," has not the ring of an uncompromising altruism or of a white, dispassionate abnegation; it is a state of inner poise and wideness which is the foundation of spiritual freedom. With that poise, in that freedom we have to do the "work that is to be done," a phrase which the Gita uses with the greatest wideness including in it all works, *sarvakarmāṇi*, and which far exceeds, though it may include, social duties or ethical obligations. What is the work to be done is not to be determined by the individual choice; nor is the right to the action and the rejection of claim to the fruit the great word of the Gita, but only a preliminary word governing the first state of the disciple when he begins ascending the hill of Yoga. It is practically superseded at a subsequent stage. For the Gita goes on to affirm emphatically that the man is not the doer of the action; it is Prakriti, it is Nature, it is the great Force with its three modes of action that works through him, and he must learn to see that it is *not* he who does the work. Therefore the "right to action" is an idea which is only valid so long as we are still under the illusion of being the doer; it must necessarily disappear from the mind like the claim to the fruit, as soon as we cease to be to our own consciousness the doer of our works. All pragmatic egoism, whether of the claim to fruits or of the right to action, is then at an end.

But the determinism of Prakriti is not the last word of the Gita. The equality of the will and the rejection of fruits are only means for entering with the mind and the heart and the understanding into the divine consciousness and living in it; and the Gita expressly says that they are to be employed as a means as long as the disciple is unable so to live or even to seek by practice the gradual development of this higher state. And what is this Divine, whom Krishna declares himself to be? It is the Purushottama beyond the Self that acts not, beyond the Prakriti that acts, foundation of the one, master of the other, the Lord of whom all is the manifestation, who even in our present subjection to Maya sits in the heart of His creatures governing the works of Prakriti, He by whom the armies on the field of Kurukshetra have already been slain while yet they live and who uses Arjuna only as an instrument or immediate occasion of this great slaughter. Prakriti is only His executive force. The disciple has to rise beyond this Force and its three modes or Gunas; he has to become *trigunātīta*. Not to her has he to surrender his actions, over which he has no longer any claim or "right", but into the being of the Supreme. Reposing his mind and understanding, heart and will in Him, with self-knowledge, with God-knowledge, with world-knowledge, with a perfect equality, a perfect devotion, an absolute self-giving, he has to do works as an offering to the Master of all self-energisings and all sacrifice. Identified in will, conscious with that consciousness, That shall decide and initiate the action. This is the solution which the Divine Teacher offers to the disciple.

## The Supreme Word of the Gita

What the great, the supreme word of the Gita is, its *mahāvākya*, we have not to seek; for the Gita itself declares it in its last utterance, the crowning note of the great diapason. "With the Lord in thy heart take refuge with all thy being; by His grace thou shalt attain to the supreme peace and the eternal status. So have I expounded to thee a knowledge more secret than that which is hidden. Further hear the most secret, the supreme word that I shall speak to thee. Become my-minded, devoted to Me, to Me do sacrifice and adoration; infallibly, thou shalt come to Me, for dear to me art thou. Abandoning all laws of conduct seek refuge in Me alone. I will release thee from all sin; do not grieve."

*

The argument of the Gita resolves itself into three great steps by which action rises out of the human into the divine plane leaving the bondage of the lower for the liberty of a higher law. First, by the renunciation of desire and a perfect equality works have to be done as a sacrifice by man as the doer, a sacrifice to a deity who is the supreme and only

Self though by him not yet realised in his own being. This is the initial step. Second, not only the desire of the fruit, but the claim to be the doer of works has to be renounced in the realisation of the Self as the equal, the inactive, the immutable principle and of all works as simply the operation of universal Force, of the Nature-Soul, Prakriti, the unequal, active, mutable power. Lastly, the supreme Self has to be seen as the supreme Purusha governing this Prakriti, of whom the soul in Nature is a partial manifestation, by whom all works are directed, in a perfect transcendence, through Nature. To him love and adoration and the sacrifice of works have to be offered; the whole being has to be surrendered to Him, and the whole consciousness raised up to dwell in this divine consciousness so that the human soul may share in His divine transcendence of Nature and of His works and act in a perfect spiritual liberty.

The first step is Karmayoga, the selfless sacrifice of works, and here the Gita's insistence is on action. The second is Jnanayoga, the self-realisation and knowledge of the true nature of the self and the world; and here the insistence is on knowledge; but the sacrifice of works continues and the path of Works becomes one with but does not disappear into the path of Knowledge. The last step is Bhaktiyoga, adoration and seeking of the supreme Self as the Divine Being, and here the insistence is on devotion; but the knowledge is not subordinated, only raised, vitalised and fulfilled, and still the sacrifice of works continues; the double path becomes the triune way of knowledge, works and devotion. And the fruit of the sacrifice, the one fruit still placed before the seeker, is attained, union with the divine Being and oneness with the supreme divine Nature.

# KURUKSHETRA

Before we can proceed, following in the large steps of the Teacher of the Gita, to watch his tracing of the triune path of man,—the path which is that of his will, heart, thought raising themselves to the Highest and into the being of that which is the supreme object of all action, love and knowledge, we must consider once more the situation from which the Gita arises, but now in its largest bearings as a type of human life and even of all world-existence. For although Arjuna is himself concerned only with his own situation, his inner struggle and the law of action he must follow, yet, as we have seen, the particular question he raises, in the manner in which he raises it, does really bring up the whole question of human life and action, what the world is and why it is and how possibly, it being what it is, life here in the world can be reconciled with life in the Spirit. And all this deep and difficult matter the Teacher insists on resolving as the very foundation of his command to an action which must proceed from a new poise of being and by the light of a liberating knowledge.

*

But what, then, is it that makes the difficulty for the man who has to take the world as it is and act in it and yet would live, within, the spiritual life? What is this aspect of existence which appals his awakened mind and brings about what the title of the first chapter of the Gita calls significantly the Yoga of the dejection of Arjuna, the dejection and discouragement felt by the human being when he is forced to face the spectacle of the universe as it really is with the veil of the ethical illusion, the illusion of self-righteousness torn from his eyes, before a higher reconciliation with himself is effected? It is that aspect which is figured outwardly in the carnage and massacre of Kurukshetra and spiritually by the vision of the Lord of all things as Time arising to devour and destroy the creatures whom it has made. This is the vision of the Lord of all existence as the universal Creator, but also the universal Destroyer, of whom the ancient Scripture can say in a ruthless image, "The sages and the heroes are his food and death is the spice of his banquet." It is one and the same truth seen first indirectly and obscurely in the facts of life and then directly and clearly in the soul's vision of that which manifests itself in life. The outward aspect is that of world-existence and human existence proceeding by struggle and slaughter; the inward aspect is that of the universal Being fulfilling himself in a vast creation and a vast destruction. Life a battle and a field of death, this is Kurukshetra; God the Terrible, this is the vision that Arjuna sees on that field of massacre.

## War and Destruction

War and destruction are not only a universal principle of our life here in its purely material aspects, but also of our mental and moral existence. It is self-evident that in the actual life of man's intellectual, social, political, moral we can take no real step forward without a struggle, a battle between what exists and lives and what seeks to exist and live and between all that stands behind either. It is impossible, at least as men and things are, to advance, to grow, to fulfil and still to observe really and utterly that principle of harmlessness which is yet placed before us as the highest and best law of conduct. We will use only soul-force and never destroy by war or any even defensive employment of physical violence? Good, though until soul-force is effective, the Asuric force in men and nations tramples down, breaks, slaughters, burns, pollutes, as we see it doing today, but then at its ease and unhindered, and you have perhaps caused as much destruction of life by your abstinence as others by resort to violence; still you have set up an ideal which may some day and at any rate ought to lead up to better things. But even soul-force, when it is effective, destroys. Only those who have used it with eyes open, know how much more terrible and destructive it is than the sword and the cannon; and only those who do not limit their view to the act and its immediate results, can see how tremendous are its after-effects, how much is eventually destroyed and with that much all the life that depended on it and fed upon it. Evil cannot perish without the destruction of much that lives by the evil, and it is no less destruction even if we personally are saved the pain of a sensational act of violence.

\*

But if we look at results, an easy optimism becomes even less possible. See the patriot dying in order that his country may be free, and mark that country a few decades after the Lord of Karma has paid the price of the blood and the suffering that was given; you shall see it in its turn an oppressor, an exploiter and conqueror of colonies and dependencies devouring others that it may live and succeed aggressively in life. The Christian martyrs perish in their thousands, setting soul-force against empire-force that Christ may conquer, Christianity prevail. Soul-force does triumph, Christianity does prevail,—but not Christ; the victorious religion becomes a militant and dominant Church and a more fanatically persecuting power than the creed and the empire which it replaced. The very religions organise themselves into powers of mutual strife and battle together fiercely to live, to grow, to possess the world.

## God as Destroyer

All which seems to show that here is an element in existence, perhaps the initial element, which we do not know how to conquer either because it cannot be conquered or because we have not looked at it with a strong and impartial gaze so as to recognise it calmly and fairly and know what it is. We must look existence in the face if our aim is to arrive at a right solution, whatever that solution may be. And to look existence in the face is to look God in the face; for the two cannot be separated, nor the responsibility for the laws of world-existence be shifted away from Him who created them or from That which constituted it. Yet here too we love to palliate and equivocate. We erect a God of Love and Mercy, a God of good, a God just, righteous and virtuous according to our own moral conceptions of justice, virtue and righteousness, and all the rest, we say, is not He or is not His, but was made by some diabolical Power which He suffered for some reason to work out its wicked will or by some dark Ahriman counterbalancing our gracious Ormuzd, or was even the fault of selfish and sinful man who has spoiled what was made originally perfect by God. As if man had created the law of death and devouring in the animal world, or that tremendous process by which Nature creates indeed and preserves but in the same step and by the same inextricable action slays and destroys. It is only a few religions which have had the courage to say without any reserve, like the Indian, that this enigmatic World-Power is one Deity, one Trinity, to lift up the image of the Force that acts in the world in the figure not only of the beneficent Durga, but of the terrible Kali in her blood-stained dance of destruction and to say, "This too is the Mother; this also know to be God; this too, if thou hast the strength, adore." And it is significant that the religion which has had this unflinching honesty and tremendous courage, has succeeded in creating a profound and wide-spread spirituality such as no other can parallel. For truth is the foundation of real spirituality and courage is its soul. *Tasyai... satyam āyatanam.*

All this is not to say that strife and destruction are the alpha and omega of existence, that harmony is not greater than war, love more the manifest divine than death or that we must not move towards the replacement of physical force by soul-force, of war by peace, of strife by union, of devouring by love, of egoism by universality, of death by immortal life. God is not only the Destroyer, but the Friend of creatures; not only the cosmic Trinity, but the Transcendent; the terrible Kali is also the loving and beneficent Mother; the lord of Kurukshetra is the divine comrade and charioteer, the attracter of beings, incarnate Krishna. And whithersoever he is driving through all the strife and clash and confusion, to whatever goal or godhead he may be attracting us, it is—no doubt of that—to some transcendence of all these aspects upon which we have been so firmly insisting. But where, how, with what kind of transcendence, under what conditions, this we have to discover; and to discover it, the first necessity is to see the world as it is, to observe and value rightly his action as it reveals itself at the start and now; afterwards the way and the goal will better reveal themselves. We must acknowledge Kurukshetra; we must submit to the law of Life by Death before we can find our way to the life immortal; we must open our eyes, with a less appalled gaze than Arjuna's, to the vision of our Lord of Time and Death and cease to deny, hate or recoil from the universal Destroyer.

# MAN AND THE BATTLE OF LIFE

## The Faith we must have

.....if we accept at all, as the Gita accepts, the existence of God, that is to say of the omnipresent, omniscient, omnipotent, yet always transcendent Being who manifests the world and Himself in the world, who is not the slave but the lord of His creative Consciousness, Nature or Force (Maya, Prakriti or Shakti), who is not baffled or thwarted in His world-conception or design by His creatures, man or devil, who does not need to justify Himself by shifting the responsibility for any part of His creation or manifestation on that which is created or manifested, then the human being has to start from a great, a difficult act of faith. Finding himself in a world which is apparently a chaos of battling powers, a clash of vast and obscure forces, a life which subsists only by constant change and death, menaced from every side by pain, suffering, evil and destruction, he has to see the omnipresent Deity in it all and conscious that of this enigma there must be a solution and beyond this Ignorance in which he dwells a Knowledge that reconciles, he has to take his stand upon this faith, "Though Thou slay me, yet will I trust in Thee."

*

A day may come, must surely come, we will say, when humanity will be ready spiritually, morally, socially for the reign of universal peace; meanwhile the aspect of battle and the nature and function of man as a fighter have to be accepted and accounted for by any practical philosophy and religion. The Gita, taking life as it is and not only as it may be in some distant future, puts the question how this aspect and function of life, which is really an aspect and function of human activity in general, can be harmonised with the spiritual existence.

## The Impulse of Renunciation

Arjuna is the Kshatriya, the rajasic man who governs his rajasic action by a high sattwic ideal. He advances to this gigantic struggle, to this Kurukshetra with the full acceptance of the joy of battle, as to "a holiday of fight", but with a proud confidence in the righteousness of his cause; he advances in his rapid chariot tearing the hearts of his enemies with the victorious clamour of his war-conch; for he wishes to look upon all these Kings of men who have come here to champion against him the cause of unrighteousness and establish as a rule of life the disregard of law, justice and truth which they would replace by the rule of a selfish and arrogant egoism. When this confidence is shattered within him, when he is smitten down from his customary attitude and mental basis of life, it is by the uprush of the tamasic quality into the rajasic man, inducing a recoil of astonishment, grief, horror, dismay, dejection, bewilderment of the mind and the war of reason against itself, a collapse towards the principle of ignorance and inertia. As a result he turns towards renunciation. Better the life of the mendicant living upon alms than this *dharma* of the Kshatriya, this battle and action culminating in undiscriminating massacre, this principle of mastery and glory and power which can only be won by destruction and bloodshed, this conquest

**35**

of blood-stained enjoyments, this vindication of justice and right by a means which contradicts all righteousness and this affirmation of the social law by a war which destroys in its process and result all that constitutes society.

*Sannyāsa* is the renunciation of life and action and of the threefold modes of Nature, but it has to be approached through one or other of the three qualities. The impulse may be tamasic, a feeling of impotence, fear, aversion, disgust, horror of the world and life; or it may be the rajasic quality tending towards tamas, an impulse of weariness of the struggle, grief, disappointment, refusal to accept any longer this vain turmoil of activity with its pains and its eternal discontent. Or the impulse may be that of rajas tending towards sattwa, the impulse to arrive at something superior to anything life can give, to conquer a higher state, to trample down life itself under the feet of an inner strength which seeks to break all bonds and transcend all limits. Or it may be sattwic, an intellectual perception of the vanity of life and the absence of any real goal or justification for this ever-cycling world-existence or else a spiritual perception of the Timeless, the Infinite, the Silent, the nameless and formless Peace beyond. The recoil of Arjuna is the tamasic recoil from action of the sattwa-rajasic man. The Teacher may confirm it in its direction, using it as a dark entry to the purity and peace of the ascetic life; or he may purify it at once and raise it towards the rare altitudes of the sattwic tendency of renunciation. In fact, he does neither. He discourages the tamasic recoil and the tendency to renunciation and enjoins the continuance of action and even of the same fierce and terrible action, but he points the disciple towards another and inner renunciation which is the real issue from his crisis and the way towards the soul's superiority to the world-Nature and yet its calm and self-possessed action in the world. Not a physical asceticism, but an inner askesis is the teaching of the Gita.

# THE CREED OF THE ARYAN FIGHTER

## The Divine Compassion

"Whence has come to thee this dejection, this stain and darkness of the soul in the hour of difficulty and peril?" asks Krishna of Arjuna. The question points to the real nature of Arjuna's deviation from his heroic qualities. There is a divine compassion which descends to us from high and for the man whose nature does not possess it, is not cast in its mould, to pretend to be the superior man, the master-man or the superman is a folly and an insolence, for he alone is the superman who most manifests the highest nature of the Godhead in humanity. This compassion observes with an eye of love and wisdom and calm strength the battle and the struggle, the strength and weakness of man, his virtues and sins, his joy and suffering, his knowledge and his ignorance, his wisdom and his folly, his aspiration and his failure and it enters into it all to help and to heal. In the saint and philanthropist it may cast itself into the mould of a plenitude of love or charity; in the thinker and hero, it assumes the largeness and the force of a helpful wisdom and strength. It is this compassion in the Aryan fighter, the soul of his chivalry, which will not break the bruised reed, but helps and protects the weak and the oppressed and the wounded and the fallen. But it is also the divine compassion that smites down the strong tyrant and the confident oppressor, not in wrath and with hatred,—for these are not the high divine qualities, the wrath of God against the sinner, God's hatred of the wicked are the fables of half-enlightened creeds, as much a fable as the eternal torture of the Hells they have invented,—but, as the old Indian spirituality clearly saw, with as much love and compassion for the strong Titan erring by his strength and slain for his sins as for the sufferer and the oppressed who have to be saved from his violence and injustice.

But such is not the compassion which actuates Arjuna in the rejection of his work and mission. That is not compassion but an impotence full of a weak self-pity, a recoil from the mental suffering which his act must entail on himself,—"I see not what shall thrust from me the sorrow that dries up the senses,"—and of all things self-pity is among the most ignoble and un-Aryan of moods. Its pity for others is also a form of self-indulgence; it is the physical shrinking of the nerves from the act of slaughter, the egoistic emotional shrinking of the heart from the destruction of the Dhritarashtrians because they are "one's own people" and without them life will be empty. This pity is a weakness of the mind and senses,—a weakness which may well be beneficial to men of a lower grade of development, who have to be weak because otherwise they will be hard and cruel; for they have to cure the harsher by the gentler forms of sensational egoism, they have to call in tamas, the debile principle, to help sattwa, the principle of light, in quelling the strength and excess of their rajasic passions. But this way is not for the developed Aryan man who has to grow not by weakness, but by an ascension from strength to strength.

## The Call of the Hero

Arjuna is the divine man, the master-man in the making and as such he has been chosen by the gods. He has a work given to him, he has God beside him in his chariot, he has the heavenly bow Gandiva in his hand, he has the champions of unrighteousness, the opponents of the divine leading of the world in his front. Not his is the right to determine what he shall do or not do according to his emotions and his passions, or to shrink from a necessary destruction by the claim of his egoistic heart and reason, or to decline his work because it will bring sorrow and emptiness to his life or because its earthly result has no value to him in the absence of the thousands who must perish. All that is a weak falling from his higher nature. He has to see only the work that must be done, *kartavyam karma*, to hear only the divine command breathed through his warrior nature, to feel only for the world and the destiny of mankind calling to him as its god-sent man to assist its march and clear its path of the dark armies that beset it.

\*

For there is continually a struggle between right and wrong, justice and injustice, the force that protects and the force that violates and oppresses, and when this has once been brought to the issue of physical strife, the champion and standard-bearer of the Right must not shake and tremble at the violent and terrible nature of the work he has to do; he must not abandon his followers or fellow-fighters, betray his cause and leave the standard of Right and Justice to trail in the dust and be trampled into mire by the blood-stained feet of the oppressor, because of a weak pity for the violent and cruel and a physical horror of the vastness of the destruction decreed. His virtue and his duty lie in battle and not in abstention from battle; it is not slaughter, but non-slaying which would here be the sin.

It is the creed of the Aryan fighter. "Know God," it says,-
"know thyself, help man; protect the Right, do without fear
or weakness or faltering thy work of battle in the world.
Thou art the eternal and imperishable Spirit, thy soul is
here on its upward path to immortality; life and death are
nothing, sorrow and wounds and suffering are nothing, for
these have to be conquered and overcome. Look not at thy
own pleasure and gain and profit, but above and around,
above at the shining summits to which thou climbest,
around at this world of battle and trial in which good and
evil, progress and retrogression are locked in stern conflict.
Men call to thee, their strong man, their hero for help; help
them, fight. Destroy when by destruction the world must
advance, but hate not that which thou destroyest, neither
grieve for all those who perish. Know everywhere the one
self, know all to be immortal souls and the body to be but
dust. Do thy work with a calm, strong and equal spirit;
fight and fall nobly or conquer mightily. For this is the work
that God and thy nature have given to thee to accomplish."

## The Thought Structure of the Gita

The whole object of the first six chapters of the Gita is to
synthetise in a large frame of Vedantic truth the two methods,
ordinarily supposed to be diverse and even opposite, of
the Sankhyas and the Yogins. The Sankhya is taken as the
starting-point and the basis; but it is from the beginning and
with a progressively increasing emphasis permeated with the
ideas and methods of Yoga and remoulded in its spirit....

In the first six chapters the Gita lays a large foundation
for its synthesis of works and knowledge, its synthesis of
Sankhya, Yoga and Vedanta.

*

The first six chapters of the Gita have been treated as a single block of teachings, its primary basis of practice and knowledge; the remaining twelve may be similarly treated as two closely connected blocks which develop the rest of the doctrine from this primary basis. The seventh to the twelfth chapters lay down a large metaphysical statement of the nature of the Divine Being, and on that foundation closely relate and synthetise knowledge and devotion, just as the first part of the Gita related and synthetised works and knowledge. The vision of the World-Purusha intervenes in the eleventh chapter, gives a dynamic turn to this stage of the synthesis and relates it vividly to works and life. Thus again all is brought powerfully back to the original question of Arjuna around which the whole exposition revolves and completes its cycle. Afterwards the Gita proceeds by the differentiation of the Purusha and Prakriti to work out its ideas of the action of the gunas, of the ascension beyond the gunas and of the culmination of desireless works with knowledge where that coalesces with Bhakti,—knowledge, works and love made one,—and it rises thence to its great finale, the supreme secret of self-surrender to the Master of Existence.

In this second part of the Gita, we come to a more concise and easy manner of statement than we have yet had. In the first six chapters, the definitions have not yet been made which give the key to the underlying truth; difficulties are being met and solved; the progress is a little laboured and moves through several involutions and returns; much is implied the bearing of which is not yet clear. Here we seem to get on to clearer ground and to lay hold of a more compact and pointed expression. But because of this very conciseness, we have to be careful always of our steps in order to avoid error and a missing of the real sense. For we are here no longer steadily on the safe ground of psychological and spiritual experience, but have to deal with intellectual statements of spiritual and often of supracosmic truth. Metaphysical statement has always this peril and uncertainty about it that it is an attempt to define to our minds what is really infinite, an attempt which has to be made, but can never be quite satisfactory, quite final or ultimate. The highest spiritual truth can be lived, can be seen, but can only be partially stated. The deeper method and language of the Upanishads with its free resort to image and symbol, its intuitive form of speech in which the hard limiting definiteness of intellectual utterance is broken down and the implications of words are allowed to roll out into an illimitable wave of suggestion, is in these realms the only right method and language. But the Gita cannot resort to this form, because it is designed to satisfy an intellectual difficulty, answers a state of mind in which the reason, the arbiter to which we refer the conflicts of our impulses and sentiments, is at war with itself and impotent to arrive at a conclusion. The reason has to be led to a truth beyond itself, but by its own means and in its own manner. Offered a spiritually psychological solution, of the data of which it has no experience, it can only be assured of its validity if it is satisfied by an intellectual statement of the truths of being upon which the solution rests.

*

The Gita in its last six chapters, in order to found on a clear and complete knowledge the way of the soul's rising out of the lower into the divine nature, restates in another form the enlightenment the Teacher has already imparted to Arjuna. Essentially it is the same knowledge, but details and relations are now made prominent and assigned their entire significance, thoughts and truths brought out in their full value that were alluded to only in passing or generally stated in the light of another purpose. Thus in the first six chapters the knowledge necessary for the distinction between the immutable self and the soul veiled in nature was accorded an entire prominence. The references to the supreme Self and Purusha were summary and not at all explicit; it was assumed in order to justify works in the world and it was affirmed to be the Master of being, but there was otherwise nothing to show what it was and its relations to the rest were not even hinted at, much less developed. The remaining chapters are devoted to the bringing out of this suppressed knowledge in a conspicuous light and strong preeminence. It is to the Lord, the Ishwara, it is to the distinction of the higher and the lower nature and to the vision of the all-originating and all-constituting Godhead in Nature, it is to the One in all beings that prominence has been assigned in the next six Adhyayas (7-12) in order to found a root-unity of works and love with knowledge. But now it is necessary to bring out more definitely the precise relations between the supreme Purusha, the immutable self, the Jiva and Prakriti in her action and her gunas. Arjuna is therefore made to put a question which shall evoke a clearer elucidation of these still ill-lighted matters. He asks to learn of the Purusha and the Prakriti; he inquires of the field of being and the knower of the field and of knowledge and the object of knowledge. Here is contained the sum of all the knowledge of self and the world that is still needed if the soul is to throw off its natural ignorance and staying its steps on a right use of knowledge, of life, of works and of its own relations with the Divine in these things ascend into unity of being with the eternal Spirit of existence.

# THE GIST OF THE KARMAYOGA

## Beyond Fear through Yoga

I have declared to you the poise of a self-liberating intelligence in Sankhya, says the divine Teacher to Arjuna. I will now declare to you another poise in Yoga. You are shrinking from the results of your works, you desire other results and turn from your right path in life because it does not lead you to them. But this idea of works and their result, desire of result as the motive, the work as a means for the satisfaction of desire, is the bondage of the ignorant who know not what works are, nor their true source, nor their real operation, nor their high utility. My Yoga will free you from all bondage of the soul to its works, *karmabandham prahāsyasi*. You are afraid of many things, afraid of sin, afraid of suffering, afraid of hell and punishment, afraid of God, afraid of this world, afraid of the hereafter, afraid of yourself. What is it that you are not afraid of at this moment, you the Aryan fighter, the world's chief hero? But this is the great fear which besieges humanity, its fear of sin and suffering now and hereafter, its fear in a world of whose true nature it is ignorant, of a God whose true being also it has not seen and whose cosmic purpose it does not understand. My Yoga will deliver you from the great fear and even a little of it will bring deliverance. When you have once set out on this path, you will find that no step is lost; every least movement will be a gain; you will find there no obstacle that can baulk you of your advance. A bold and absolute promise and one to which the fearful and hesitating mind beset and stumbling in all its paths cannot easily lend an assured trust; nor is the

**45**

large and full truth of it apparent unless with these first words of the message of the Gita, we read also the last, "Abandon all laws of conduct and take refuge in Me alone; I will deliver you from all sin and evil; do not grieve."

## Beyond Desire

It is the upward and inward orientation of the intelligent will that we must resolutely choose with a settled concentration and perseverance, *vyavasāya*; we must fix it firmly in the calm self-knowledge of the Purusha. The first movement must be obviously to get rid of desire which is the whole root of the evil and suffering; and in order to get rid of desire, we must put an end to the cause of desire, the rushing out of the senses to seize and enjoy their objects. We must draw them back when they are inclined thus to rush out, draw them away from their objects,—as the tortoise draws in his limbs into the shell, so these into their source, quiescent in the mind, the mind quiescent in intelligence, the intelligence quiescent in the soul and its self-knowledge, observing the action of Nature but not object to it not desiring any thing that the objective life can give.

It is not an external asceticism, the physical renunciation of the objects of sense that I am teaching, suggests Krishna immediately to avoid a misunderstanding which is likely at once to arise. Not the renunciation of the Sankhyas or the austerities of the rigid ascetic with his fasts, his maceration of the body, his attempt to abstain even from food; that is not the self-discipline or the abstinence which I mean, for I speak of an inner withdrawal, a renunciation of desire. The embodied soul, having a body, has to support it normally by food for its normal physical action; by abstention from food it simply removes from itself the physical contact with the object of sense, but does not get rid of the inner relation which makes that contact hurtful. It retains the pleasure of the sense in the object, the *rasa*, the liking and disliking,—for *rasa* has two sides; the soul must, on the contrary, be capable of enduring the physical contact without suffering inwardly this sensuous reaction. Otherwise there is *nivṛtti,* cessation of the object, *viṣayā viniartante,* but no subjective cessation, no *nivṛtti* of the mind; but the senses are of the mind, subjective, and subjective cessation of the *rasa* is the only real sign of mastery. But how is this desireless contact with objects, this unsensuous use of the senses possible? It is possible, *param dṛṣṭstavā,* by the vision of the supreme,—*param,* the Soul, the Purusha, — and by living in the Yoga, in union or oneness of the whole subjective being with that, through the Yoga of the intelligence; for the one Soul is calm, satisfied in its own delight, and that delight free from duality can take, once we see this supreme thing in us and fix the mind and will on that, the place of the sensuous object-ridden pleasures and repulsions of the mind. This is the true way of liberation.

Certainly self-discipline, self-control is never easy. All intelligent human beings know that they must exercise some control over themselves and nothing is more common than this advice to control the senses; but ordinarily it is only advised imperfectly and practised imperfectly in the most limited and insufficient fashion. Even, however, the sage, the man of clear, wise and discerning soul who really labours to acquire complete self-mastery finds himself hurried and carried away by the senses. That is because the mind naturally lends itself to the senses; it observes the objects of sense with an inner interest, settles upon them and makes them the object of absorbing thought for the intelligence and of strong interest for the will. By that attachment comes, by attachment desire, by desire distress, passion and anger when the desire is not satisfied or is thwarted or opposed, and by passion the soul is obscured, the intelligence and will forget to see and be seated in the calm observing soul; there is a fall from the memory of one's true self, and by that lapse the intelligent will is also obscured, destroyed even. For, for the time being, it no longer exists to our memory of ourselves, it disappears in a cloud of passion; we become passion, wrath, grief and cease to be self and intelligence and will. This then must be prevented and all the senses brought utterly under control; for only by an absolute control of the senses can the wise and calm intelligence be firmly established in its proper seat.

This cannot be done perfectly by the act of the intelligence itself, by a merely mental self-discipline; it can only be done by Yoga with something which is higher than itself and in which calm and self-mastery are inherent. And this Yoga can only arrive at its success by devoting, by consecrating, by giving up the whole self to the Divine, "to Me", says Krishna; for the Liberator is within us, but it is not our mind, nor our intelligence, nor our personal will,— they are only instruments. It is the Lord in whom, as we are told in the end, we have utterly to take refuge. And for that we must at first make him the object of our whole being and keep in soul-contact with him. This is the sense of the phrase "he must sit firm in Yoga, wholly given up to Me"; but as yet it is the merest passing hint after the manner of the Gita, three words only which contain in seed the whole gist of the highest secret yet to be developed, *yukta āsīta matparaḥ.*

## Desireless Action and Sacrifice

The difficulty is this, how, our nature being what it is and desire the common principle of its action, is it possible to institute a really desireless action? For what we call ordinarily disinterested action is not really desireless; it is simply a replacement of certain smaller personal interests by other larger desires which have only the appearance of being impersonal, virtue, country, mankind. All action, moreover, as Krishna insists, is done by the Gunas of Prakriti, by our nature; in acting according to the Shastra we are still acting according to our nature, – even if this Shastric action is not, as it usually is, a mere cover for our desires, prejudices, passions, egoisms, our personal, national, sectarian vanities, sentiments and preferences; but even otherwise, even at the purest, still we obey a choice of our nature, and if our nature were different and the Gunas acted on our intelligence and will in some other combination, we would not accept the Shastra, but live according to our pleasure or our intellectual notions or else break free from the social law to live the life of the solitary or the ascetic. We cannot become impersonal by obeying something outside ourselves, for we cannot so get outside ourselves; we can only do it by rising to the highest in ourselves, into our free Soul and Self which is the same and one in all and has therefore no personal interests, to the Divine in our being who possesses Himself transcendent of cosmos and is therefore not bound by His cosmic works or His individual action. That is what the Gita teaches and desirelessness is only a means to this end, not an aim in itself. Yes, but how is it to be brought about? By doing all works with sacrifice as the only object, is the reply of the divine Teacher. "By doing works otherwise than for sacrifice, this world of men is in bondage to works;

for sacrifice practise works, O son of Kunti, becoming free from all attachment." It is evident that all works and not merely sacrifice and social duties can be done in this spirit; any action may be done either from the ego-sense narrow or enlarged or for the sake of the Divine. All being and all action of Prakriti exist only for the sake of the Divine; from that it proceeds, by that it endures, to that it is directed. But so long as we are dominated by the ego-sense, we cannot perceive or act in the spirit of this truth, but act for the satisfaction of the ego and in the spirit of the ego, other than for sacrifice. Egoism is the knot of the bondage. By acting Godwards, without any thought of ego, we loosen this knot and finally arrive at freedom.

## Beyond the Gunas

The three qualitative modes of Nature are inextricably intertwined in all cosmic existence. Tamas, the principle of inertia, is a passive and inert nescience which suffers all shocks and contacts without any effort of mastering response and by itself would lead to a disintegration of the whole action of the energy and a radical dispersion of substance. But it is driven by the kinetic power of rajas and even in the nescience of Matter is met and embraced by an innate though unpossessed preserving principle of harmony and balance and knowledge. Material energy appears to be tamasic in its basic action, *jada,* nescient, mechanic and in movement disintegrative. But it is dominated by a huge force and impulsion of mute rajasic kinesis which drives it, even in and even by its dispersion and disintegration, to build and create and again by a sattwic ideative element in its apparently inconscient force which is always imposing a harmony and preservative order on the two opposite tendencies. Rajas, the principle of creative endeavour and motion and impulsion in Prakriti, kinesis, *pravṛtti,* so seen in Matter, appears more evidently as a conscious or half-conscious passion of seeking and desire and action in the dominant character of Life,—for that passion is the nature of all vital existence. And it would lead by itself in its own nature to a persistent but always mutable and unstable life and activity and creation without any settled result. But met on one side by the disintegrating power of tamas with death and decay and inertia, its ignorant action is on the other side of its functioning settled and harmonised and sustained by the power of Sattwa, subconscient in the lower forms of life, more and more conscient in the emergence of mentality, most conscious in the effort of the evolved intelligence figuring as will and reason in the fully developed mental being. Sattwa, the principle of understanding knowledge and of according assimilation, measure and equilibrium, which by itself would lead only to some lasting concord of fixed and luminous harmonies, is in the motions of this world impelled to follow the mutable strife and action of the eternal kinesis and constantly overpowered or hedged in by the forces of inertia and nescience. This is the appearance of a world governed by the interlocked and mutually limited play of the three qualitative modes of Nature.

The Gita applies this generalised analysis of the universal Energy to the psychological nature of man in relation to his bondage to Prakriti and the realisation of spiritual freedom. Sattwa, it tells us, is by the purity of its quality a cause of light and illumination and by virtue of that purity, it produces no disease or morbidity or suffering in the nature. When into all the doors in the body there comes a flooding of light, as if the doors and windows of a closed house were opened to sunshine, a light of understanding, perception and knowledge,—when the intelligence is alert and illumined, the senses quickened, the whole mentality satisfied and full of brightness and the nervous being calmed and filled with an illumined ease and clarity, *prasāda*, one should understand that there has been a great increase and uprising of the sattwic guna in the nature. For knowledge and a harmonious ease and pleasure and happiness are the characteristic results of sattwa. The pleasure that is sattwic is not only that contentment which an inner clarity of satisfied will and intelligence brings with it, but all delight and content produced by the soul's possession of itself in light or by an accord or an adequate and truthful adjustment between the regarding soul and the surrounding Nature and her offered objects of desire and perception.

Rajas, again, the Gita tells us, has for its essence attraction of liking and longing. Rajas is a child of the attachment of the soul to the desire of objects; it is born from the nature's thirst for an unpossessed satisfaction. It is therefore full of unrest and fever and lust and greed and excitement, a thing of seeking impulsions, and all this mounts in us when the middle Guna increases. It is the force of desire which motivate all ordinary personal initiative of action and all that movement of stir and seeking and propulsion in our nature which is the impetus towards action and works, *pravṛtti*. Rajas, then, is evidently the kinetic force in the modes of Nature. Its fruit is the lust of action, but also grief, pain, all kinds of suffering; for it has no right possession of its object—desire; in fact implies non-possession—and even its pleasure of acquired possession is troubled and unstable because it has not clear knowledge and does not know how to possess nor can it find the secret of accord and right enjoyment. All the ignorant and passionate seeking of life belongs to the rajasic mode of Nature.

Tamas, finally, is born of inertia and ignorance and its fruit too is inertia and ignorance. It is the darkness of Tamas which obscures knowledge and causes all confusion and delusion. Therefore it is the opposite of Sattwa, for the essence of Sattwa is enlightenment, *prakāśa*, and the essence of Tamas is absence of light, nescience, *aprakāśa*. But Tamas brings incapacity and negligence of action as well as the incapacity and negligence of error, inattention and misunderstanding or non-understanding; indolence, languor and sleep belong to this Guna. Therefore it is the opposite too of Rajas; for the essence of Rajas is movement and impulsion and kinesis, *pravṛtti*, but the essence of Tamas is inertia, *pravṛtti*. Tamas is inertia of nescience and inertia of inaction, a double negative.

These three qualities of Nature are evidently present and active in all human beings and none can be said to be quite devoid of one and another or free from any one of the three; none is cast in the mould of one Guna to the exclusion of the others. All men have in them in whatever degree the rajasic impulse of desire and activity and the sattwic boon of light and happiness, some balance, some adjustment of mind to itself and its surroundings and objects, and all have their share of tamasic incapacity and ignorance or nescience. But these qualities are not constant in any man in the quantitative action of their force or in the combination of their elements; for they are variable and in a continual state of mutual impact, displacement and interaction. Now one leads, now another increases and predominates, and each subjects us to its characteristic action and consequences. Only by a general and ordinary predominance of one or other of the qualities can a man be said to be either sattwic or rajasic or tamasic in his nature; but this can only be a general and not an exclusive or absolute description. The three qualities are a triple power which by their interaction determine the character and disposition, and through that and its various motions the actions of the natural man. But this triple power is at the same time a triple cord of bondage. "The three Gunas born of Prakriti," says the Gita "bind in the body the imperishable dweller in the body." In a certain sense we can see at once that there must be this bondage in following the action of the Gunas; for they are all limited by their finite of quality and operation and cause limitation. Tamas is on both its sides an incapacity and therefore very obviously binds to limitation. Rajasic desire as an initiator of action is a more positive power, but still we can see well enough that desire with its limiting and engrossing hold on man must always be a bondage. But how does Sattwa, the power of knowledge and happiness, become a chain? It so becomes because it is a principle of mental nature, a principle of limited and limiting knowledge and of a happiness which depends upon right following or attainment of this or that object or else on particular states of the mentality, on a light of mind which can be only a more or less clear twilight. Its pleasure can only be a passing intensity or a qualified ease. Other is the infinite spiritual knowledge and the free self-existent delight of our spiritual being.

But then there is the question, how does our infinite and imperishable spirit, even involved in Nature, come thus to confine itself to the lower action of Prakriti and undergo this bondage and how is it not, like the supreme spirit of which it is a portion, free in its infinity even while enjoying the self-limitations of its active evolution? The reason, says the Gita, is our attachment to the Gunas and to the result of their workings. Sattwa, it says, attaches to happiness, rajas attaches to action, Tamas covers up the knowledge and attaches to negligence of error and inaction. Or again, "Sattwa binds by attachment to knowledge and attachment to happiness, rajas binds the embodied spirit by attachment to works, Tamas binds by negligence and indolence and sleep." In other words, the soul by attachment to the enjoyment of the Gunas and their results concentrates its consciousness on the lower and outward action of life, mind and body in Nature, imprisons itself in the form of these things and becomes oblivious of its own greater consciousness behind in the spirit, unaware of the free power and scope of the liberating Purusha. Evidently, in order to be liberated and perfect, we must get back from these things, away from the Gunas and above them and return to the power of that free spiritual consciousness above Nature.

But this would seem to imply a cessation of all doing, since all natural action is done by the Gunas, by Nature through her modes. The soul cannot act by itself, it can only act through Nature and her modes. And yet the Gita, while it demands freedom from the modes, insists upon the necessity of action. Here comes in the importance of its insistence on the abandonment of the fruits; for it is the desire of the fruits which is the most potent cause of the soul's bondage, and by abandoning it, the soul can be free in action. Ignorance is the result of tamasic action, pain the consequence of rajasic works, pain of reaction, disappointment, dissatisfaction or transience, and therefore in attachment to the fruits of this kind of activity attended as they are with these undesirable accompaniments there is no profit. But of works rightly done the fruit is pure and sattwic, the inner result is knowledge and happiness. Yet attachment even to these pleasurable things must be entirely abandoned, first, because in the mind they are limited and limiting forms and, second, because, since Sattwa is constantly entangled with and besieged by Rajas and Tamas which may at any moment overcome it, there is a perpetual insecurity in their tenure. But, even if one is free from any clinging to the fruit, there may be an attachment to the work itself, either for its own sake, the essential rajasic bond, or owing to a lax subjection to the drive of Nature, the tamasic, or for the sake of the attracting rightness of the thing done, which is the sattwic attaching cause powerful on the virtuous man or the man of knowledge. And here evidently the resource is in that other injunction of the Gita, to give up the action itself to the Lord of works and be only a desireless and equal-minded instrument of his will. To see that the modes of Nature are the whole agency and cause of our works and to know and turn to that which is supreme above the Gunas, is the way to rise above the lower nature. Only so can we attain to the movement and status of the Divine, *mad-bhāva*, by which free from subjection to birth and death and their concomitants, decay, old age and suffering, the liberated soul shall enjoy in the end immortality and all that is eternal.

## The Purpose of Action

"Thou shouldst do works regarding also the holding together of the peoples, *lokasaṁgraham evāpi saṁpaśyam kartum arhasi.* Whatsoever the Best doeth, that the lower kind of man puts into practice; the standard he creates, the people follows. O son of Pritha, I have no work that I need to do in all the three worlds, I have nothing that I have not gained and have yet to gain, and I abide verily in the paths of action," *varta eva ca karmaṇi,—eva* implying, I abide in it and do not leave it as the Sannyasin thinks himself bound to abandon works. "For if I did not abide sleeplessly in the paths of action, men follow in every way my path, these peoples would sink to destruction if I did not work and I should be the creator of confusion and slay these creatures. As those who know not act with attachment to the action, he who knows should act without attachment, having for his motive to hold together the peoples. He should not create a division of their understanding in the ignorant who are attached to their works; he should set them to all actions, doing them himself with knowledge and in Yoga." There are few more important passages in the Gita than these seven striking couplets.

But let us clearly understand that they must not be interpreted, as the modern pragmatic tendency concerned much more with the present affairs of the world than with any high and far-off spiritual possibility seeks to interpret them, as no more than a philosophical and religious justification of social service, patriotic, cosmopolitan and humanitarian effort and attachment to the hundred eager social schemes and dreams which attract the modern intellect. It is not the rule of a large moral and intellectual altruism which is here announced, but that of a spiritual unity with God and with this world of beings who dwell in him and in whom he dwells. It is not an injunction to subordinate the individual to society and humanity or immolate egoism on the altar of the human collectivity, but to fulfil the individual in God and to sacrifice the ego on the one true altar of the all-embracing Divinity. The Gita moves on a plane of ideas and experiences higher than those of the modern mind which is at the stage indeed of a struggle to shake off the coils of egoism, but is still mundane in its outlook and intellectual and moral rather than spiritual in its temperament. Patriotism, cosmopolitanism, service of society, collectivism, humanitarianism, the ideal or religion of humanity are admirable aids towards our escape from our primary condition of individual, family, social, national egoism into a secondary stage in which the individual realises, as far as it can be done on the intellectual, moral and emotional level,—on that level he cannot do it entirely in the right and perfect way, the way of the integral truth of his being,—the oneness of his existence with the existence of other beings. But the thought of the Gita reaches beyond to a tertiary condition of our developing self-consciousness towards which the secondary is only a partial stage of advance.

\*

To exalt oneself out of the lower imperfect prakriti, *traiguṇyamayi māyā*, into unity with the divine being, consciousness and nature, *madbhāvam āgatāḥ*, is the object of the Yoga. But when this object is fulfilled, when the man is in the Brahmic status and sees no longer with the false egoistic vision himself and the world, but sees all beings in the Self, in God, and the Self in all beings, God in all beings, what shall be the action,—since action there still is,—which results from that seeing, and what shall be the cosmic or individual motive of all his works? It is the question of Arjuna, but answered from a standpoint other than that from which Arjuna had put it. The motive cannot be personal desire on the intellectual, moral, emotional level, for that has been abandoned,—even the moral motive has been abandoned, since the liberated man has passed beyond the lower distinction of sin and virtue, lives in a glorified purity beyond good and evil. It cannot be the spiritual call to his perfect self-development by means of disinterested works, for the call has been answered, the development is perfect and fulfilled. His motive of action can only be the holding together of the peoples, *cikīrṣur lokasaṁgraham.* This great march of the peoples towards a far-off divine ideal has to be held together, prevented from falling into the bewilderment, confusion and utter discord of the understanding which would lead to dissolution and destruction and to which the world moving forward in the night or dark twilight of ignorance would be too easily prone if it were not held together, conducted, kept to the great lines of its discipline by the illumination, by the strength, by the rule and example, by the visible standard and the invisible influence of its Best. The best, the individuals who are in advance of the general line and above the general level of the collectivity, are the natural leaders of mankind, for it is they who can point to the race both the way they must follow and the standard or ideal they have to keep to or to attain. But the divinised man is the Best in no ordinary sense of the word and his influence, his example must have a power which that of no ordinarily superior man can exercise. What example then shall he give? What rule or standard shall he uphold?

In order to indicate more perfectly his meaning, the divine Teacher, the Avatar gives his own example, his own standard to Arjuna. "I abide in the path of action," he seems to say, "the path that all men follow; thou too must abide in action. In the way I act, in that way thou too must act. I am above the necessity of works, for I have nothing to gain by them; I am the Divine who possess all things and all beings in the world and I am myself beyond the world as well as in it and I do not depend upon anything or anyone in all the three worlds for any object; yet I act. This too must be thy manner and spirit of working. I, the

Divine, am the rule and the standard; it is I who make the path in which men tread; I am the way and the goal. But I do all this largely, universally, visibly in part, but far more invisibly; and men do not really know the way of my workings. Thou, when thou knowest and seest, when thou hast become the divinized man, must be the individual power of God, the human yet divine example, even as I am in my avatars. Most men dwell in the ignorance, the God-seer dwells in the knowledge; but let him not confuse the minds of men by a dangerous example, rejecting in his superiority the works of the world; let him not cut short the thread of action before it is spun out, let him not perplex and falsify the stages and gradations of the ways I have hewn. The whole range of human action has been decreed by me with a view to the progress of man from the lower to the higher nature, from the apparent undivine to the conscious Divine. The whole range of human works must be that in which the God-knower shall move. All individual, all social action, all the works of the intellect, the heart and the body are still his, not any longer for his own separate sake, but for the sake of God in the world, of God in all beings and that all those beings may move forward, as he has moved, by the path of works towards the discovery of the Divine in themselves. Outwardly his actions may not seem to differ essentially from theirs; battle and rule as well as teaching and thought, all the various commerce of man with man may fall in his range; but the spirit in which he does them must be very different, and it is that spirit which by its influence shall be the great attraction drawing men upwards to his own level, the great lever lifting the mass of men higher in their ascent."

# THE DIVINE WORKER

## The Sign of Divine Work

To Attain to the divine birth,—a divinising new birth of the soul into a higher consciousness,—and to do divine works both as a means towards that before it is attained and as an expression of it after it is attained, is then all the Karmayoga of the Gita. The Gita does not try to define works by any outward signs through which it can be recognisable to an external gaze, measurable by the criticism of the world; it deliberately renounces even the ordinary ethical distinctions by which men seek to guide themselves in the light of the human reason. The signs by which it distinguishes divine works are all profoundly intimate and subjective; the stamp by which they are known is invisible, spiritual, supra-ethical.

They are recognisable only by the light of the soul from which they come. For, it says, "what is action and what is inaction, as to this even the sages are perplexed and deluded," because, judging by practical, social, ethical, intellectual standards, they discriminate by accidentals and do not go to the root of the matter; "I will declare to thee that action by the knowledge of which thou shalt be released from all ills. One has to understand about action as well as to understand about wrong action and about inaction one has to understand; thick and tangled is the way of works." Action in the world is like a deep forest, *gahana*, through which man goes stumbling as best he can, by the light of the ideas of his time, the standards of his personality, his environment, or rather of many times, many personalities, layers of thought and ethics from many social stages all inextricably confused together, temporal and conventional amidst all their claim to absoluteness and immutable truth, empirical and irrational in spite of their aping of right reason. And finally, the sage seeking in the midst of it all a highest foundation of fixed law and an original truth finds himself obliged to raise the last supreme question, whether all action and life itself are not a delusion and a snare and whether cessation from action, *akarma*, is not the last resort of the tired and disillusioned human soul. But, says Krishna, in this matter even the sages are perplexed and deluded. For by action, by works, not by inaction comes the knowledge and the release.

## The First Sign

What then is the solution? What is that type of works by which we shall be released from the ills of life, from this doubt, this error, this grief, from this mixed, impure and baffling result even of our purest and best-intentioned acts, from these million forms of evil and suffering? No outward distinctions need be made, is the reply; no work the world needs, be shunned; no limit or hedge set around our human activities; on the contrary, all actions should be done, but from a soul in Yoga with the Divine, *yuktaḥ kṛtsna-karma-kṛt. Akarma*, cessation from action is not the way; the man who has attained the insight of the highest reason, perceives that such inaction is itself a constant action, a state subject to the workings of Nature and her qualities. The mind that takes refuge in physical inactivity, is still under the delusion that it and not Nature is the doer of works; it has mistaken inertia for liberation; it does not see that even in what seems absolute inertia greater than that of the stone or clod, Nature is at work, keeps unimpaired her hold. On the contrary in the full flood of action the soul is free from its works, is not the doer, not bound by what is done, and he who lives in the freedom of the soul, not in the bondage of the modes of Nature, alone has release from works. This is what the Gita clearly means when it says that he who in action can see inaction and can see action still continuing in cessation from works, is the man of true reason and discernment among men. This saying hinges upon the Sankhya distinction between Purusha and Prakriti, between the free inactive soul, eternally calm, pure and unmoved in the midst of works, and ever active Nature operative as much in inertia and cessation as in the overt turmoil of her visible hurry of labour. This is the knowledge which the highest effort of the discriminating reason, the *buddhi*, gives to us, and therefore whoever possesses it is the truly rational and discerning man, *sa buddhimān manuṣyeṣu,*—not the perplexed thinker who judges life and works by the external, uncertain and impermanent distinctions of the lower reason. Therefore the liberated man is not afraid of action, he is a large and universal doer of all works, *kṛtsna-karma-kṛt*; not as others do them in subjection to Nature, but poised in the silent calm of the soul, tranquilly in Yoga with the Divine. The Divine is the lord of his works, he is only their channel through the instrumentality of his nature conscious of and subject to her Lord. By the flaming intensity and purity of this knowledge, all his works are burned up as in a fire and his mind remains without any stain or disfiguring mark from them, calm, silent, unperturbed, white and clean and pure. To do all in this liberating knowledge, without the personal egoism of the doer, is the first sign of the divine worker.

## The Second Sign

The second sign is freedom from desire; for where there is not the personal egoism of the doer, desire becomes impossible; it is starved out, sinks for want of a support, dies of inanition. Outwardly the liberated man seems to undertake works of all kinds like other men, on a larger scale perhaps with a more powerful will and driving-force, for the might of the divine will works in his active nature; but from all his inceptions and undertakings the inferior concept and nether will of desire is entirely banished, *sarve samārambhāḥ kāmasaṁkalpavarjitāḥ*. He has abandoned all attachment to the fruits of his works, and where one does not work for the fruit, but solely as an impersonal instrument of the Master of works, desire can find no place,—not even the desire to serve successfully, for the fruit is the Lord's and determined by him and not by the personal will and effort, or to serve with credit and to the Master's satisfaction, for the real doer is the Lord himself and all glory belongs to a form of his Shakti missioned in the nature and not to the limited human personality. The human mind and soul of the liberated man does nothing, *na kiñcit karoti*; even though through his nature he engages in action, it is the Nature, the executive Shakti, it is the conscious Goddess governed by the divine Inhabitant who does the work.

It does not follow that the work is not to be done perfectly, with success, with a right adaptation of means to ends: on the contrary, a perfect working is easier to action done tranquilly in Yoga than to action done in the blindness of hopes and fears, lamed by the judgments of the stumbling reason, running about amidst the eager trepidations of the hasty human will: Yoga, says the Gita elsewhere, is the true skill in works, *yogaḥ karmasu kauśalam*. But all this is done impersonally by the action of a great universal light and power operating through the individual nature. The Karmayogin knows that the power given to him will be adapted to the fruit decreed, the divine thought behind the work equated with the work he has to do, the will in him,—which will not be wish or desire, but an impersonal drive of conscious power directed towards an aim not his own,—subtly regulated in its energy and direction by the divine wisdom. The result may be success, as the ordinary mind understands it, or it may seem to that mind to be defeat and failure; but to him it is always the success intended, not by him, but by the all-wise manipulator of action and result, because he does not seek for victory, but only for the fulfilment of the divine will and wisdom which works out its ends through apparent failure as well as and often with greater force than through apparent triumph. Arjuna, bidden to fight, is assured of victory; but even if certain defeat were before him, he must still fight because that is the present work assigned to him as his immediate share in the great sum of energies by which the divine will is surely accomplished.

## The Third Sign

The liberated man has no personal hopes; he does not seize on things as his personal possessions; he receives what the divine Will brings him, covets nothing, is jealous of none: what comes to him he takes without repulsion and without attachment; what goes from him he allows to depart into the whirl of things without repining or grief or sense of loss. His heart and self are under perfect control; they are free from reaction and passion, they make no turbulent response to the touches of outward things. His action is indeed a purely physical action, *śārīram kevalam karma*; for all else comes from above, is not generated on the human plane, is only a reflection of the will, knowledge, joy of the divine Purushottama. Therefore he does not stress on doing and its objects bring about in his mind and heart any of those reactions which we call passion and sin. For sin consists not at all in the outward deed, but in an impure reaction of the personal will, mind and heart which accompanies it or causes it; the impersonal, the spiritual is always pure, *apāpaviddham*, and gives to all that it does its own inalienable purity. This spiritual impersonality is a third sign of the divine worker. All human souls, indeed, who have attained to a certain greatness and largeness are conscious of an impersonal Force or Love or Will and Knowledge working through them, but they are not free from egoistic reactions, sometimes violent enough, of their human personality. But this freedom the liberated soul has attained; for he has cast his personality into the impersonal, where it is no longer his, but is taken up by the divine Person, the Purushottama, who uses all finite qualities infinitely and freely and is bound by none. He has become a soul and ceased to be a sum of natural qualities; and such appearance of personality as remains for the operations of Nature, is something unbound, large, flexible, universal; it is a free mould for the Infinite, it is a living mask of the Purushottama.

## The Fourth Sign

The result of this knowledge, this desirelessness and this impersonality is a perfect equality in the soul and the nature. Equality is the fourth sign of the divine worker. He has, says the Gita, passed beyond the dualities; he is *dvandvātīta*. We have seen that he regards with equal eyes, without any disturbance of feeling, failure and success, victory and defeat; but not only these, all dualities are in him surpassed and reconciled. The outward distinctions by which men determine their psychological attitude towards the happenings of the world, have for him only a subordinate and instrumental meaning. He does not ignore them, but he is above them. Good happening and evil happening, so all-important to the human soul subject to desire, are to the desireless divine soul equally welcome since by their mingled strand are worked out the developing forms of the eternal good. He cannot be defeated, since all for him is moving towards the divine victory in the Kurukshetra of Nature, *dharmakṣetre kurukṣetre*, the field of doings which is the field of the evolving Dharma, and every turn of the conflict has been designed and mapped by the foreseeing eye of the Master of the battle, the Lord of works and Guide of the dharma. Honour and dishonour from men cannot move him, nor their praise nor their blame; for he has a greater clear-seeing judge and another standard for his action, and his motive admits no dependence upon worldly rewards. Arjuna the Kshatriya prizes naturally honour and reputation and is right in shunning disgrace and the name of coward as worse than death; for to maintain the point of honour and the standard of courage in the world is part of his dharma: but Arjuna the liberated soul need care for none of these things, he has only to know the *kartavyam karma*, the work which the supreme Self demands from him, and to do that and leave the result to the Lord of his actions. He has passed even beyond that distinction of sin and virtue which is so all-important to the human soul while it is struggling to minimise the hold of its egoism and lighten the heavy and violent yoke of its passions,—the liberated has risen above these struggles and is seated firmly in the purity of the witnessing and enlightened soul. Sin has fallen away from him, and not a virtue acquired and increased by good action and impaired or lost by evil action, but the inalienable and unalterable purity of a divine and selfless nature is the peak to which he has climbed and the seat upon which he is founded. There the sense of sin and the sense of virtue have no starting-point or applicability.

Arjuna, still in the ignorance, may feel in his heart the call of right and justice and may argue in his mind that abstention from battle would be a sin entailing responsibility for all the suffering that injustice and oppression and the evil karma of the triumph of wrong bring upon men and nations, or he may feel in his heart the recoil from violence and slaughter and argue in his mind that all shedding of blood is a sin which nothing can justify. Both of these attitudes would appeal with equal right to virtue and reason and it would depend upon the man, the circumstances and the time which of these might prevail in his mind or before the eyes of the world. Or he might simply feel constrained by his heart and his honour to support his friends against his enemies, the cause of the good and just against the cause of the evil and oppressive. The liberated soul looks beyond these conflicting standards; he sees simply what the supreme Self demands from him as needful for the maintenance or for the bringing forward of the evolving Dharma. He has no personal ends to serve, no personal loves and hatreds to satisfy, no rigidly fixed standard of action which opposes its rock-line to the flexible advancing march of the progress of the human race or stands up defiant against the call of the Infinite. He has no personal enemies to be conquered or slain, but sees only men who have been brought up against him by circumstances and the will in things to help by their opposition the march of destiny. Against them he can have no wrath or hatred; for wrath and hatred are foreign to the divine nature. The Asura's desire to break and slay what opposes him, the Rakshasa's grim lust of slaughter are impossible to his calm and peace and his all-embracing sympathy and understanding. He has no wish to injure, but on the contrary a universal friendliness and compassion, *maitraḥ karuṇa eva ca*: but this compassion is that of a divine soul overlooking men, embracing all other souls in himself, not the shrinking of the heart and the nerves and the flesh which is the ordinary human form of pity: nor does he attach a supreme importance to the life of the body, but looks beyond to the life of the soul and attaches to the other only an instrumental value. He will not hasten to slaughter and strife, but if war comes in the wave of the Dharma, he will accept it with a large equality and a perfect understanding and sympathy for those whose power and pleasure of domination he has to break and whose joy of triumphant life he has to destroy. For in all he sees two things, the Divine inhabiting every being equally, the varying manifestation unequal only in its temporary circumstances. In the animal and man, in the dog, the unclean outcaste and the learned and virtuous Brahmin, in the saint and the sinner, in the indifferent and the friendly and the hostile, in those who love him and benefit and those who hate him and afflict, he sees himself, he sees God and has at heart for all the same equal kindliness, the same divine affection. Circumstances may determine the outward clasp or the outward conflict, but can never affect his equal eye, his open heart, his inner embrace of all. And in all his actions, there will be the same principle of soul, a perfect equality, and the same principle of work, the will of the Divine in him active for the need of the race in its gradually developing advance towards the Godhead.

## The Fifth Sign

Again, the sign of the divine worker is that which is central to the divine consciousness itself, a perfect inner joy and peace which depends upon nothing in the world for its source or its continuance; it is innate, it is the very stuff of the soul's consciousness, it is the very nature of divine being. The ordinary man depends upon outward things for his happiness; therefore he has desire; therefore he has anger and passion, pleasure and pain, joy and grief; therefore he measures all things in the balance of good fortune and evil fortune. None of these things can affect the divine soul; it is ever satisfied without any kind of dependence, *nitya-tṛpto nirāśrayaḥ*; for its delight, its divine ease, its happiness, its glad light are eternal within, ingrained in itself, *ātmaratiḥ, antaḥsukho'ntarārāmas tathāntarjyotir eva yaḥ*. What joy it takes in outward things is not for their sake, not for things which it seeks in them and can miss, but for the self in them, for their expression of the Divine, for that which is eternal in them and which it cannot miss. It is without attachment to their outward touches, but finds everywhere the same joy that it finds in itself, because its self is theirs, has become one self with the self of all beings, because it is united with the one and equal Brahman in them through all their differences, *brahmayogayuktātmā, sarvabhūtātmabhūtātmā*. It does not rejoice in the touches of the pleasant or feel anguish in the touches of the unpleasant; neither the wounds of things, nor the wounds of friends, nor the wounds of enemies can disturb the firmness of its outgazing mind or bewilder its receiving heart; this soul is in its nature, as the Upanishad puts it, *avraṇam*, without wound or scar. In all things it has the same imperishable Ananda, *sukham akṣayam aśnute*.

That equality, impersonality, peace, joy, freedom do not depend on so outward a thing as doing or not doing works. The Gita insists repeatedly on the difference between the inward and the outward renunciation, *tyāga* and *sannyāsa*. The latter, it says, is valueless without the former, hardly possible even to attain without it, and unnecessary when there is the inward freedom. In fact *tyāga* itself is the real and sufficient Sannyasa. "He should be known as the eternal Sannyasin who neither hates nor desires; free from the dualities he is happily and easily released from all bondage." The painful process of outward Sannyasa, *duḥkham āptum*, is an unnecessary process. It is perfectly true that all actions, as well as the fruit of action, have to be given up, to be renounced, but inwardly, not outwardly, not into the inertia of Nature, but to the Lord in sacrifice, into the calm and joy of the Impersonal from whom all action proceeds without disturbing his peace. The true Sannyasa of action is the reposing of all works on the Brahman. "He who, having abandoned attachment, acts reposing (or founding) his works on the Brahman, *brahmaṇyādhāya karmāṇi*, is not stained by sin even as water clings not to the lotus-leaf." Therefore the Yogins first "do works with the body, mind, understanding, or even merely with the organs of action, abandoning attachment, for self-purification, *saṅgam tyaktvātmaśuddhaye*. By abandoning attachment to the fruits of works the soul in union with Brahman attains to peace of rapt foundation in Brahman, but the soul not in union is attached to the fruit and bound by the action of desire." The foundation, the purity, the peace once attained, the embodied soul perfectly controlling its nature, having renounced all its actions by the mind, inwardly, not outwardly, "sits in its nine-gated city neither doing nor causing to be done." For this soul is the one impersonal Soul in all, the all-pervading Lord, *prabhu, vibhu*, who, as the impersonal, neither creates the works of the world, nor the mind's idea of being the doer, *na kartṛtvan na karmāṇi*, nor the coupling of works to their fruits, the chain of cause and effect. All that is worked out by the Nature in the man, *svabhāva*, his principle of self-becoming, as the word literally means. The all-pervading Impersonal accepts neither the sin nor the virtue of any: these are things created by the ignorance in the creature, by his egoism of the doer, by his ignorance of his highest self, by his involution in the operations of Nature, and when the self-knowledge within him is released from this dark envelope, that knowledge lights up like a sun the real self within him; he knows himself then to be the soul supreme above the instruments of Nature. Pure, infinite, inviolable, immutable, he is no longer affected; no longer does he imagine himself to be modified by her workings. By complete identification with the Impersonal he can, too, release himself from the necessity of returning by birth into her movement.

## The Sixth Sign

And yet this liberation does not at all prevent him from acting. Only, he knows that it is not he who is active, but the modes, the qualities of Nature, her triple Gunas.

"The man who knows the principles of things thinks, his mind in Yoga (with the inactive Impersonal), 'I am doing nothing'; when he sees, hears, touches, smells, eats, moves, sleeps, breathes, speaks, takes, ejects, opens his eyes or closes them, he holds that it is only the senses acting upon the objects of the senses." He himself, safe in the immutable, unmodified soul, is beyond the grip of the three Gunas, *trigunātīta*; he is neither sattwic, rajasic nor tamasic; he sees with a clear untroubled spirit the alternations of the natural modes and qualities in his action, their rhythmic play of light and happiness, activity and force, rest and inertia. This superiority of the calm soul observing its action but not involved in it, this *traigunātītya*, is also a high sign of the divine worker. By itself the idea might lead to a doctrine of the mechanical determinism of Nature and the perfect aloofness and irresponsibility of the soul; but the Gita effectively avoids this fault of an insufficient thought by its illumining supertheistic idea of the Purushottama. It makes it clear that it is not in the end Nature which mechanically determines its own action; it is the will of the Supreme which inspires her; he who has already slain the Dhritarashtrians, he of whom Arjuna is only the human instrument, a universal Soul, a transcendent Godhead is the master of her labour. The reposing of works in the Impersonal is a means of getting rid of the personal egoism of the doer, but the end is to give up all our actions to that great Lord of all, *sarvabhūtamaheśvara*. "With a consciousness identified with the Self, renouncing all thy actions into *may savāni karmāni samnyasyādhyātmacetasā*, freed from personal hopes and desires, from the thought of 'I' and 'mine', delivered from the fever of the soul, fight," work, do my will in the world. The Divine motivates, inspires, determines the entire action; the human soul impersonal in the Brahman is the pure and silent channel of his power; that power in the Nature executes the divine movement. Such only are the works of the liberated soul, *muktasya karma*, for in nothing does he act from a personal inception; such are the actions of the accomplished Karmayogin. They rise from a free spirit and disappear without modifying it, like waves that rise and disappear on the surface of conscious, immutable depths. *Gata-saṅgasya muktasya jñānāvasthita-cetasaḥ, yajñāyācarataḥ karma samagraṁ pravilīyate.*

# AVATARHOOD

## Two Aspects of Divine Birth

For there are two aspects of the divine birth; one is a descent, the birth of God in humanity, the Godhead manifesting itself in the human form and nature, the eternal Avatar; the other is an ascent, the birth of man into the Godhead, man rising into the divine nature and consciousness, *madbhāvam āgataḥ*; it is the being born anew in a second birth of the soul. It is that new birth which Avatarhood and the upholding of the Dharma are intended to serve. This double aspect in the Gita's doctrine of Avatarhood is apt to be missed by the cursory reader satisfied, as most are, with catching a superficial view of its profound teachings, and it is missed too by the formal commentator petrified in the rigidity of the schools. Yet it is necessary, surely, to the whole meaning of the doctrine. Otherwise the Avatar idea would be only a dogma, a popular superstition, or an imaginative or mystic deification of historical or legendary supermen, not what the Gita makes all its teaching, a deep philosophical and religious truth and an essential part of or step to the supreme mystery of all, *rahasyam uttamam*.

If there were not this rising of man into the Godhead to be helped by the descent of God into humanity, Avatarhood for the sake of the Dharma would be an otiose phenomenon, since mere Right, mere justice or standards of virtue can always be upheld by the divine omnipotence through its ordinary means, by great men or great movements, by the life and work of sages and kings and religious teachers, without any actual incarnation. The Avatar comes as the manifestation of the divine nature in the human nature, the apocalypse of its Christhood, Krishnahood, Buddhahood, in order that the human nature may by moulding its principle, thought, feeling, action, being on the lines of that Christhood, Krishnahood, Buddhahood transfigure itself into the divine. The law, the Dharma which the Avatar establishes is given for that purpose chiefly; the Christ, Krishna, Buddha stands in its centre as the gate, he makes through himself the way men shall follow. That is why each Incarnation holds before men his own example and declares of himself that he is the way and the gate; he declares too the oneness of his humanity with the divine being, declares that the Son of Man and the Father above from whom he has descended are one, that Krishna in the human body, *mānuṣīm tanum āśritam*, and the supreme Lord and Friend of all creatures are but two revelations of the same divine Purushottama, revealed there in his own being, revealed here in the type of humanity.

*

In the ordinary human birth the Nature-aspect of the universal Divine assuming humanity prevails; in the incarnation the God-aspect of the same phenomenon takes its place. In the one he allows the human nature to take possession of his partial being and to dominate it; in the other, he takes possession of his partial type of being and its nature and divinely dominates it. Not by evolution or ascent like the ordinary man, the Gita seems to tell us, not by a growing into the divine birth, but by a direct descent into the stuff of humanity and a taking up of its moulds.

## The Purpose of Avatarhood

But it is to assist that ascent or evolution the descent is made or accepted; that the Gita makes very clear. It is, we might say, to exemplify the possibility of the Divine manifest in the human being, so that man may see what that is and take courage to grow into it. It is also to leave the influence of that manifestation vibrating in the earth-nature and the soul of that manifestation presiding over its upward endeavour. It is to give a spiritual mould of divine manhood into which the seeking soul of the human being can cast itself. It is to give a dharma, a religion,—not a mere creed, but a method of inner and outer living,—a way, a rule and law of self-moulding by which he can grow towards divinity. It is too, since this growth, this ascent is no mere isolated and individual phenomenon, but like all in the divine world-activities a collective business, a work and the work for the race, to assist the human march, to hold it together in its great crises, to break the forces of the downward gravitation when they grow too insistent, to uphold or restore the great dharma of the Godward law in man's nature, to prepare even, however far off, the kingdom of God, the victory of the seekers of light and perfection, *sādhūnām*, and the overthrow of those who fight for the continuance of the evil and the darkness. All these are recognised objects of the descent of the Avatar, and it is usually by his work that the mass of men seek to distinguish him and for that that they are ready to worship him. It is only the spiritual who see that this external Avatarhood is a sign, in the symbol of a human life, of the eternal inner Godhead making himself manifest in the field of their own human mentality and corporeality so that they can grow into unity with that and be possessed by it. The divine manifestation of a Christ, Krishna, Buddha in external humanity has for its inner truth the same manifestation of the eternal Avatar within in our own inner humanity. That which has been done in the outer human life of earth, may be repeated in the inner life of all human beings.

## The Avatar – a Dual Phenomenon

This doctrine is a hard saying, a difficult thing for the human reason to accept; and for an obvious reason, because of the evident humanity of the Avatar. The Avatar is always a dual phenomenon of divinity and humanity; the Divine takes upon himself the human nature with all its outward limitations and makes them the circumstances, means, instruments of the divine consciousness and the divine power, a vessel of the divine birth and the divine works. But so surely it must be, since otherwise the object of the Avatar's descent is not fulfilled; for that object is precisely to show that the human birth with all its limitations can be made such a means and instrument of the divine birth and divine works, precisely to show that the human type of consciousness can be compatible with the divine essence of consciousness made manifest, can be converted into its vessel, drawn into nearer conformity with it by a change of its mould and a heightening of its powers of light and love and strength and purity; and to show also how it can be done. If the Avatar were to act in an entirely supernormal fashion, this object would not be fulfilled. A merely supernormal or miraculous Avatar would be a meaningless absurdity; not that there need be an entire absence of the use of supernormal powers such as Christ's so-called miracles of healing, for the use of supernormal powers is quite a possibility of human nature; but there need not be that at all, nor in any case is it the root of the matter, nor would it at all do if the life were nothing else but a display of supernormal fireworks. The Avatar does not come as a thaumaturgic magician, but as the divine leader of humanity and the exemplar of a divine humanity. Even human sorrow and physical suffering he must assume and use so as to show, first, how that suffering may be a means of redemption,—as did Christ,—secondly, to show how, having been assumed by the divine soul in the human nature, it can also be overcome in the same nature,—as did Buddha. The rationalist who would have cried to Christ, "If thou art the Son of God, come down from the cross," or points out sagely that the Avatar was not divine because he died and died too by disease,—as a dog dieth,—knows not what he is saying: for he has missed the root of the whole matter. Even, the Avatar of sorrow and suffering must come before there can be the Avatar of divine joy; the human limitation must be assumed in order to show how it can be overcome; and the way and the extent of the overcoming, whether internal only or external also, depends upon the stage of the human advance; it must not be done by a non-human miracle.

## The Work of the Avatar

It is these things that condition and determine the work of the Avatar. In the Buddhistic formula, the disciple takes refuge from all that opposes his liberation in three powers, the *dharma*, the *saṁgha*, the Buddha. So in Christianity we have the law of Christian living, the Church and Christ. These three are always the necessary elements of the work of the Avatar. He gives a dharma, a law of self-discipline by which to grow out of the lower into the higher life and which necessarily includes a rule of action and of relations with our fellowmen and other beings, endeavour in the eightfold path or the law of faith, love and purity or any other such revelation of the nature of the divine in life. Then because every tendency in man has its collective as well as its individual aspect, because those who follow one way are naturally drawn together into spiritual companionship and unity, he establishes the sangha, the fellowship and union of those whom his personality and his teaching unite. In Vaishnavism there is the same trio, *bhāgavata*, *bhakta*, *bhagavān*,—the *bhāgavat*, which is the law of the Vaishnava dispensation of adoration and love, the *bhakta* representing the fellowship of those in whom that law is manifest, *bhagavān*, the divine Lover and Beloved in whose being and nature the divine law of love is founded and fulfils itself. The Avatar represents this third element, the divine personality, nature and being who is the soul of the Dharma and the *saṁgha*, informs them with himself, keeps them living and draws men towards the felicity and the liberation.

In the teaching of the Gita, which is more catholic and complex than other specialised teachings and disciplines, these things assume a larger meaning. For the unity here is the all-embracing Vedantic unity by which the soul sees all in itself and itself in all and makes itself one with all beings. The Dharma is therefore the taking up of all human relations into a higher divine meaning; starting from the established ethical, social and religious rule which binds together the whole community in which the God-seeker lives, it lifts it up by informing it with the Brahmic consciousness; the law it gives is the law of oneness, of equality, of liberated, desireless, God-governed action, of God-knowledge and self-knowledge enlightening and drawing to itself all the nature and all the action, drawing it towards divine being and divine consciousness, and of God-love as the supreme power and crown of the knowledge and the action. The idea of companionship and mutual aid in God-love and God-seeking which is at the basis of the idea of the *saṁgha* or divine fellowship, is brought in when the Gita speaks of the seeking of God through love and adoration, but the real *saṁgha* of this teaching is all humanity. The whole world is moving towards this dharma, each man according to his capacity,—"it is my path that men follow in every way,"—and the God-seeker, making himself one with all, making their joy and sorrow and all their life his own, the liberated made already one self with all beings, lives in the life of humanity, lives for the one Self in humanity, for God in all beings, acts for *lokasaṁgraha*, for the maintaining of all in their Dharma and the Dharma, for the maintenance of their growth in all its stages and in all its paths towards the Divine. For the Avatar here, though he is manifest in the name and form of Krishna, lays no exclusive stress on this one form of his human birth, but on that which it represents, the Divine, the Purushottama, of whom all Avatars are the human births, of whom all forms and names of the Godhead worshipped by men are the figures. The way declared by Krishna here is indeed announced as the way by which man can reach the real knowledge and the real liberation, but it is one that is inclusive of all paths and not exclusive. For the Divine takes up into his universality all Avatars and all teachings and all dharmas. The Gita lays stress upon the struggle of which the world is the theatre, in its two aspects, the inner struggle and the outer battle. In the inner struggle the enemies are within, in the individual, and the slaying of desire, ignorance, egoism is the victory. But there is an outer struggle between the powers of the Dharma and the Adharma in the human collectivity. The former is supported by the divine, the godlike nature in man, and by those who represent it or strive to realise it in human life, the latter by the Titanic or demoniac, the Asuric and Rakshasic nature whose head is a violent egoism, and by those who represent and strive to satisfy it. This is the war of the Gods and Titans, the symbol of which the old Indian literature is full, the struggle of the Mahabharata of which Krishna is the central figure being often represented in that image; the Pandavas who fight for the establishment of the kingdom of the Dharma, are the sons of the Gods, their powers in human form, their adversaries are incarnations of the Titanic powers, they are Asuras. This outer struggle too the Avatar comes to aid, directly or indirectly, to destroy the reign of the Asuras, the evil-doers, and in them depress the power they represent and to restore the oppressed ideals of the Dharma. He comes to bring nearer the kingdom of heaven on earth in the collectivity as well as to build the kingdom of heaven within in the individual human soul.

\*

The inner fruit of the Avatar's coming is gained by those who learn from it the true nature of the divine birth and the divine works and who, growing full of him in their consciousness and taking refuge in him with their whole being, *manmayā mām upāśritāḥ* purified by the realising force of their knowledge and delivered from the lower nature, attain to the divine being and divine nature, *madbhāvam*. The Avatar comes to reveal the divine nature in man above this lower nature and to show what are the divine works, free, unegoistic, disinterested, impersonal, universal, full of the divine light, the divine power and the divine love. He comes as the divine personality which shall fill the consciousness of the human being and replace the limited egoistic personality, so that it shall be liberated out of ego into infinity and universality, out of birth into immortality. He comes as the divine power and love which calls men to itself, so that they may take refuge in that and no longer in the insufficiency of their human wills and the strife of their human fear, wrath and passion, and liberated from all this unquiet and suffering may live in the calm and bliss of the Divine. Nor does it matter essentially in what form and name or putting forward what aspect of the Divine he comes; for in all ways, varying with their nature, men are following the path set to them by the Divine which will in the end lead them to him and the aspect of him which suits their nature is that which they can best follow when he comes to lead them; in whatever way men accept, love and take joy in God, in that way God accepts, loves and takes joy in man. *Ye yathā mām prapadyante tāms tathaiva bhajāmyaham.*

# THE VISION OF THE WORLD-SPIRIT

## Time the Destroyer

The vision of the universal Purusha is one of the best known and most powerfully poetic passages in the Gita, but its place in the thought is not altogether on the surface. It is evidently intended for a poetic and revelatory symbol and we must see how it is brought in and for what purpose and discover to what it points in its significant aspects before we can capture its meaning. It is invited by Arjuna in his desire to see the living image, the visible greatness of the unseen Divine, the very embodiment of the Spirit and Power that governs the universe. He has heard the highest spiritual secret of existence, that all is from God and all is the Divine and in all things God dwells and is concealed and can be revealed in every finite appearance. The illusion which so persistently holds man's sense and mind, the idea that things at all exist in themselves or for themselves apart from God or that anything subject to Nature can be self-moved and self-guided, has passed from him,—that was the cause of his doubt and bewilderment and refusal of action. Now he knows what is the sense of the birth and passing away of existences. He knows that the imperishable greatness of the divine conscious Soul is the secret of all these appearances. All is a Yoga of this great eternal Spirit in things and all happenings are the result and expression of that Yoga; all Nature is full of the secret Godhead and in labour to reveal him in her. But he would see too the very form and body of this Godhead, if that be possible. He has heard of his attributes and understood the steps and ways of his self-revelation; but now he asks of this Master of the Yoga to discover his very imperishable Self to the eye of Yoga. Not, evidently, the formless silence of his actionless immutability, but the Supreme from whom is all energy and action, of whom forms are the masks, who reveals his force in the Vibhuti,—the Master of works, the Master of knowledge and adoration, the Lord of Nature and all her creatures. For this greatest all-comprehending vision he is made to ask because it is so, from the Spirit revealed in the universe, that he must receive the command to his part in the world-action.

*

What thou hast to see, replies the Avatar, the human eye cannot grasp,—for the human eye can see only the outward appearances of things or make out of them separate symbol forms, each of them significant of only a few aspects of the eternal Mystery. But there is a divine eye, an inmost seeing, by which the supreme Godhead in his Yoga can be beheld and that eye I now give to thee. Thou shalt see, he says, my hundreds and thousands of divine forms, various in kind, various in shape and hue; thou shalt see the Adityas and the Rudras and the Maruts and the Aswins; thou shalt see many wonders that none has beheld; thou shalt see today the whole world related and unified in my body and whatever else thou willest to behold. This then is the keynote, the central significance. It is the vision of the One in the many, the Many in the One,—and all are the One. It is this vision that to the eye of the divine Yoga liberates, justifies, explains all that is and was and shall be. Once seen and held, it lays the shining axe of

God at the root of all doubts and perplexities and annihilates all denials and oppositions. It is the vision that reconciles and unifies. If the soul can arrive at unity with the Godhead in this vision,—Arjuna has not yet done that, therefore we find that he has fear when he sees,—all even that is terrible in the world loses its terror. We see that it too is an aspect of the Godhead and once we have found his meaning in it, not looking at it by itself alone, we can accept the whole of existence with an all-embracing joy and a mighty courage, go forward with sure steps to the appointed work and envisage beyond it the supreme consummation. The soul admitted to the divine knowledge which beholds all things in one view, not with a divided, partial and therefore bewildered seeing, can make a new discovery of the world and all else that it wills to see, *yac cānyad draṣṭum icchasi*; it can move on the basis of this all-relating and all-unifying vision from revelation to completing revelation.

The supreme Form is then made visible. It is that of the infinite Godhead whose faces are everywhere and in whom are all the wonders of existence, who multiplies unendingly all the many marvellous revelations of his being, a world-wide Divinity seeing with innumerable eyes, speaking from innumerable mouths, armed for battle with numberless divine uplifted weapons, glorious with divine ornaments of beauty, robed in heavenly raiment of deity, lovely with garlands of divine flowers, fragrant with divine perfumes. Such is the light of this body of God as if a thousand suns had risen at once in heaven. The whole world multitudinously divided and yet unified is visible in the body of the God of Gods. Arjuna sees him, God magnificent and beautiful and terrible, the Lord of souls who has manifested in the glory and greatness of his spirit this wild and monstrous and orderly and wonderful and sweet and terrible world, and overcome with marvel and joy and fear he bows down and adores with words of awe and with clasped hands the tremendous vision. "I see" he cries "all the gods in thy body, O God, and different companies of beings, Brahma the creating lord seated in the Lotus, and the Rishis and the race of the divine Serpents. I see numberless arms and bellies and eyes and faces, I see thy infinite forms on every side, but I see not thy end nor thy middle nor thy beginning, O Lord of the universe, O Form universal. I see thee crowned and with thy mace and thy discus, hard to discern because thou art a luminous mass of energy on all sides of me, an encompassing blaze, a sun-bright fire-bright Immeasurable. Thou art the supreme Immutable whom we have to know, thou art the high foundation and abode of the universe, thou art the imperishable guardian of the eternal laws, thou art the sempiternal soul of existence." But in the greatness of this vision there is too the terrific image of the Destroyer. This Immeasurable without end or middle or beginning is he in whom all things begin and exist and end. This Godhead who embraces the worlds with his numberless arms and destroys with his million hands, whose eyes are suns and moons, has a face of blazing fire and is ever burning up the whole universe with the flame of his energy. The form of him is  fierce and marvellous, and alone it fills all the regions and occupies the whole space between earth and heaven. The companies of the gods enter it, afraid, adoring; the Rishis and the Siddhas crying "May there be peace and weal" praise it with many praises; the eyes of Gods and Titans and Giants are fixed on it in amazement. It has enormous burning eyes; it has mouths that gape to devour, terrible with many tusks of destruction; it has faces like the fires of Death and Time. The kings and the captains and the heroes on both sides of the world-battle are hastening into its tusked and terrible jaws and some are seen with crushed and bleeding heads caught between its teeth of power; the nations are rushing to destruction with helpless speed into its mouths of flame like many rivers hurrying in their course towards the ocean or like moths that cast themselves on a kindled fire. With those burning mouths, the Form of Dread is licking all the regions around; the whole world is full of his burning energies and baked in the fierceness of his lustres. The world and its nations are shaken and in anguish with the terror of destruction and Arjuna shares in the trouble and panic around him; troubled and in pain is the soul within him and he finds no peace or gladness. He cries to the dreadful Godhead, "Declare to me who thou art that wearest this form of fierceness. Salutation to thee, O thou great Godhead, turn thy heart to grace. I would know who thou art who wast from the beginning, for I know not the will of thy workings."

## God as Death

This last cry of Arjuna indicates the double intention in the vision. This is the figure of the supreme and universal Being, the Ancient of Days who is for ever, *sanātanam purusam purāṇam*, this is he who for ever creates, for Brahma the Creator is one of the Godheads seen in his body, he who keeps the world always in existence, for he is the guardian of the eternal laws, but who is always too destroying in order that he may new-create, who is Time, who is Death, who is Rudra the Dancer of the calm and awful dance, who is Kali with her garland of skulls trampling naked in battle and flecked with the blood of the slaughtered Titans, who is the cyclone and the fire and the earthquake and pain and famine and revolution and ruin and the swallowing ocean. And it is this last aspect of him which he puts forward at the moment. It is an aspect from which the mind in men willingly turns away and ostrich-like hides its head so that perchance, not seeing, it may not be seen by the Terrible. The weakness of the human heart wants only fair and comforting truths or in their absence pleasant fables; it will not have the truth in its entirety because there is much that is not clear and pleasant and comfortable, but hard to understand and harder to bear. The raw religionist, the superficial optimistic thinker, the sentimental idealist, the man at the mercy of his sensations and emotions agree in twisting away from the sterner conclusions, the harsher and fiercer aspects of universal existence. Indian religion has been ignorantly reproached for not sharing in this general game of hiding, because on the contrary it has built and placed before it the terrible as well as the sweet and beautiful symbols of the Godhead. But it is the depth and largeness of its long thought and spiritual experience that prevent it from feeling or from giving countenance to these feeble shrinkings.

Indian spirituality knows that God is Love and Peace and calm Eternity,—the Gita which presents us with these terrible images, speaks of the Godhead who embodies himself in them as the lover and friend of all creatures. But there is too the sterner aspect of his divine government of the world which meets us from the beginning, the aspect of destruction, and to ignore it is to miss the full reality of the divine Love and Peace and Calm and Eternity and even to throw on it an aspect of partiality and illusion, because the comforting exclusive form in which it is put is not borne out by the nature of the world in which we live. This world of our battle and labour is a fierce dangerous destructive devouring world in which life exists precariously and the soul and body of man move among enormous perils, a world in which by every step forward, whether we will it or no, something is crushed and broken, in which every breath of life is a breath too of death. To put away the responsibility for all that seems to us evil or terrible on the shoulders of a semi-omnipotent Devil, or to put it aside as part of Nature, making an unbridgeable opposition between world-nature and God-Nature, as if Nature were independent of God, or to throw the responsibility on man and his sins, as if he had a preponderant voice in the making of this world or could create anything against the will of God, are clumsily comfortable devices in which the religious thought of India has never taken refuge. We have to look courageously in the face of the reality and see that it is God and none else who has made this world in his being and that so he has made it. We have to see that Nature devouring her children, Time eating up the lives of creatures, Death universal and ineluctable and the violence of the Rudra forces in man and Nature are also the supreme Godhead in one of his cosmic figures. We have to see that God the bountiful and prodigal creator, God the helpful, strong and benignant preserver is also God the devourer and destroyer. The torment of the couch of pain and evil on which we are racked is his touch as much as happiness and sweetness and pleasure. It is only when we see with the eye of the complete union and feel this truth in the depths of our being that we can entirely discover behind that mask too the calm and beautiful face of the all-blissful Godhead and in this touch that tests our imperfection the touch of the friend and builder of the spirit in man. The discords of the worlds are God's discords, and it is only by accepting and proceeding through them that we can arrive at the greater concords of his supreme harmony, the summits and thrilled vastnesses of his transcendent and his cosmic Ananda.

*

The problem raised by the Gita and the solution it gives demand this character of the vision of the World-Spirit. It is the problem of a great struggle, ruin and massacre which has been brought about by the all-guiding Will and in which the eternal Avatar himself has descended as the charioteer of the protagonist in the battle. The seer of the vision is himself the protagonist, the representative of the battling soul of man who has to strike down tyrant and oppressive powers that stand in the path of his evolution and to establish and enjoy the kingdom of a higher right and nobler law of being. Perplexed by the terrible aspect of the catastrophe in which kindred smite at kindred, whole nations are to perish and society itself seems doomed to sink down in a pit of confusion and anarchy, he has shrunk back, refused the task of destiny and demanded of his divine Friend and Guide why he is appointed to so dreadful a work, *kim karmaṇi ghore mām niyojasyasi*. He has been shown then how individually to rise above the apparent character of whatever work he may do, to see that Nature the executive force is the doer of the work, his natural being the instrument, God the master of Nature and of works to whom he must offer them without desire or egoistic choice as a sacrifice. He has been shown too that the Divine who is above all these things and untouched by them, yet manifests himself in man and Nature and their action and that all is a movement in the cycles of this divine manifestation. But now when he is put face-to-face with the embodiment of this truth, he sees in it magnified by the image of the divine greatness this aspect of terror and destruction and is appalled and can hardly bear it. For why should it be thus that the All-spirit manifests himself in Nature? What is the significance of this creating and devouring flame that is mortal existence, this world-wide struggle, these constant disastrous revolutions, this labour and anguish and travail and perishing of creatures? He puts the ancient question and breathes the eternal prayer, "Declare to me who art thou that comest to us in this form of fierceness. I would know who art thou who wast from the beginning, for I know not the will of thy workings. Turn thy heart to grace."

Destruction, replies the Godhead, is the will of my workings with which I stand here on this field of Kurukshetra, the field of the working out of the Dharma, the field of human action,—as we might symbolically translate the descriptive phrase, *dharmakṣetre kurukṣetre*,—a world-wide destruction which has come in the process of the Time-Spirit. I have a foreseeing purpose which fulfils itself infallibly and no participation or abstention of any human being can prevent, alter or modify it; all is done by me already in My eternal eye of will before it can at all be done by man upon earth. I as Time have to destroy the old structures and to build up a new, mighty and splendid kingdom. Thou as a human instrument of the divine Power and Wisdom hast in this struggle which thou canst not prevent to battle for the right and slay and conquer its opponents. Thou too, the human soul in Nature, hast to enjoy in Nature the fruit given by Me, the empire of right and justice. Let this be sufficient for thee,—to be one with God in thy soul, to receive his command, to do his will, to see calmly a supreme purpose fulfilled in the world. "I am Time the waster of the peoples arisen and increased whose will in my workings is here to destroy the nations. Even without thee all these warriors shall be not, who are ranked in the opposing armies. Therefore arise, get thee glory, conquer thy enemies and enjoy an opulent kingdom. By me and none other already even are they slain, do thou become the occasion only, O Savyasachin. Slay, by me who are slain, Drona, Bhishma, Jayadratha, Karna and other heroic fighters; be not pained and troubled. Fight, thou shalt conquer the adversary in the battle." The fruit of the great and terrible work is promised and prophesied, not as a fruit hungered for by the individual,—for to that there is to be no attachment,—but as the result of the divine will, the glory and success of the thing to be done accomplished, the glory given by the Divine to himself in his Vibhuti. Thus is the final and compelling command to action given to the protagonist of the world-battle.

## God of Love behind the Mask of Death

Even while the effects of the terrible aspect of this vision are still upon him, the first words uttered by Arjuna after the Godhead has spoken are eloquent of a greater uplifting and reassuring reality behind this face of death and this destruction. "Rightly and in good place," he cries, "O Krishna, does the world rejoice and take pleasure in thy name, the Rakshasas are fleeing from thee in terror to all the quarters and the companies of the Siddhas bow down before thee in adoration. How should they not do thee homage, O great Spirit? For thou art the original Creator and Doer of works and greater even than creative Brahma. O thou Infinite, O thou Lord of the gods, O thou abode of the universe, thou art the Immutable and thou art what is and is not and thou art that which is the Supreme. Thou art the ancient Soul and the first and original Godhead and the supreme resting-place of this All; thou art the knower and that which is to be known and the highest status; O infinite in form, by thee was extended the universe. Thou art Yama and Vayu and Agni and Soma and Varuna and Prajapati, father of creatures, and the great-grandsire. Salutation to thee a thousand times over and again and yet again salutation, in front and behind and from every side, for thou art each and all that is. Infinite in might and immeasurable in strength of action thou pervadest all and art every one."

But this supreme universal Being has lived here before him with the human face, in the mortal body, the divine Man, the embodied Godhead, the Avatar, and till now he has not known him. He has seen the humanity only and has treated the Divine as a mere human creature. He has not pierced through the earthly mask to the Godhead of which the humanity was a vessel and a symbol, and he prays now for that Godhead's forgiveness of his unseeing carelessness and his negligent ignorance. "For whatsoever I have spoken to thee in rash vehemence, thinking of thee only as my human friend and companion, 'O Krishna, O Yadava, O comrade,' not knowing this thy greatness, in negligent error or in love, and for whatsoever disrespect was shown by me to thee in jest, on the couch and the seat and in the banquet, alone or in thy presence, I pray forgiveness from thee the immeasurable. Thou art the father of all this world of the moving and unmoving; thou art one to be worshipped and the most solemn object of veneration. None is equal to thee, how then another greater in all the three worlds, O incomparable in might? Therefore I bow down before thee and prostrate my body and I demand grace of thee the adorable Lord. As a father to his son, as a friend to his friend and comrade, as one dear with him he loves, so shouldst thou, O Godhead, bear with me. I have seen what never was seen before and I rejoice, but my mind is troubled with fear. O Godhead, show me that other form of thine. I would see thee even as before crowned and with thy mace and discus. Assume thy four-armed shape, O thousand-armed, O Form universal."

*

From the first words there comes the suggestion that the hidden truth behind these terrifying forms is a reassuring, a heartening and delightful truth. There is something that makes the heart of the world to rejoice and take pleasure in the name and nearness of the Divine. It is the profound sense of that which makes us see in the dark face of Kali the face of the Mother and to perceive even in the midst of destruction the protecting arms of the Friend of creatures, in the midst of evil the presence of a pure unalterable Benignity and in the midst of death the Master of Immortality. From the terror of the King of the divine action the Rakshasas, the fierce giant powers of darkness, flee destroyed, defeated and overpowered. But the Siddhas, but the complete and perfect who know and sing the names of the Immortal and live in the truth of his being, bow down before every form of Him and know what every form enshrines and signifies. Nothing has real need to fear except that which is to be destroyed, the evil, the ignorance, the veilers in Night, the Rakshasa powers. All the movement and action of Rudra the Terrible is towards perfection and divine light and completeness.

For this Spirit, this Divine is only in outward form the Destroyer, Time who undoes all these finite forms: but in himself he is the Infinite, the Master of the cosmic Godheads, in whom the world and all its action are securely seated. He is the original and ever originating Creator, one greater than that figure of creative Power called Brahma which he shows to us in the form of things as one aspect of his trinity, creation chequered by a balance of preservation and destruction. The real divine creation is eternal; it is the Infinite manifested sempiternally in finite things, the Spirit who conceals and reveals himself for ever in his innumerable infinity of souls and in the wonder of their actions and in the beauty of their forms. He is the eternal Immutable; he is the dual appearance of the Is and Is-not, of the manifest and the never manifested, of things that were and seem to be no more, are and appear doomed to perish, shall be and shall pass. But what he is beyond all these is That, the Supreme, who holds all things mutable in the single eternity of a Time to which all is ever present. He possesses his immutable self in a timeless eternity of which Time and creation are an ever extending figure.

*

The Godhead in answer to Arjuna's prayer reassumes his own normal Narayana image, *svakam rūpam*, the desired form of grace and love and sweetness and beauty. But first he declares the incalculable significance of the other mighty Image which he is about to veil. "This that thou now seest," he tells him, "is My supreme shape, My form of luminous energy, the universal, the original which none but thou amongst men has yet seen. I have shown it by My self-Yoga. For it is an image of My very Self and Spirit, it is the very Supreme self-figured in cosmic existence and the soul in perfect Yoga with Me sees it without any trembling of the nervous parts or any bewilderment and confusion of the mind, because he descries not only what is terrible and overwhelming in its appearance, but also its high and reassuring significance. And thou also shouldst so envisage it without fear, without confusion of mind, without any sinking of the members; but since the lower nature in thee is not yet prepared to look upon it with that high strength and tranquillity, I will reassume again for thee My Narayana figure in which the human mind sees isolated and toned to its humanity the calm, helpfulness and delight of a friendly Godhead. The greater Form"—and this is repeated again after it has disappeared—"is only for the rare highest souls. The gods themselves ever desire to look upon it. It cannot be won by Veda or austerities or gifts or sacrifice; it can be seen, known, entered into only by that bhakti which regards, adores and loves Me alone in all things."

But what then is the uniqueness of this Form by which it is lifted so far beyond cognizance that all the ordinary endeavour of human knowledge and even the inmost austerity of its spiritual effort are insufficient, unaided, to reach the vision? It is this that man can know by other means this or that exclusive aspect of the one existence, its individual, cosmic or world-excluding figures, but not this greatest reconciling Oneness of all the aspects of the Divinity in which at one and the same time and in one and the same vision all is manifested, all is exceeded and all is consummated. For here transcendent, universal and individual Godhead, Spirit and Nature, Infinite and finite, space and time and timelessness, Being and Becoming, all that we can strive to think and know of the Godhead, whether of the absolute or the manifested existence, are wonderfully revealed in an ineffable oneness. This vision can be reached only by the absolute adoration, the love, the intimate unity that crowns at their summit the fullness of works and knowledge. To know, to see, to enter into it, to be one with this supreme form of the Supreme becomes then possible, and it is that end which the Gita proposes for its Yoga. There is a supreme consciousness through which it is possible to enter into the glory of the Transcendent and contain in him the immutable Self and all mutable Becoming,—it is possible to be one with all, yet above all, to exceed world and yet embrace the whole nature at once of the cosmic and the supracosmic Godhead. This is difficult indeed for limited man imprisoned in his mind and body: but, says the Godhead, "be a doer of my works, accept me as the supreme being and object, become my bhakta, be free from attachment and without enmity to all existences; for such a man comes to me." In other words superiority to the lower nature, unity with all creatures, oneness with the cosmic Godhead and the Transcendence, oneness of will with the Divine in works, absolute love for the One and for God in all,—this is the way to that absolute spiritual self-exceeding and that unimaginable transformation.

# THE YOGA OF DIVINE LOVE

## Four Types of Bhaktas

It is bhakti with knowledge which the Gita demands from the disciple and it regards all other forms of devotion as good in themselves but still inferior; they may do well by the way, but they are not the thing at which it aims in the soul's culmination. Among those who have put away the sin of the rajasic egoism and are moving towards the Divine, the Gita distinguishes between four kinds of bhaktas. There are those who turn to him as a refuge from sorrow and suffering in the world, *ārta*. There are those who seek him as the giver of good in the world, *arthārthī*. There are those who come to him in the desire for knowledge, *jijñāsu*. And lastly, there are those who adore him with knowledge, *jñānī*. All are approved by the Gita, but only on the last does it lay the seal of its complete sanction. All these movements without exception are high and good, *udārāḥ sarva evaite*, but the bhakti with knowledge excels them all, *viśiṣyate*. We may say that these forms are successively the bhakti of the vital-emotional and affective nature,[1] that of the practical and dynamic nature, that of the reasoning intellectual nature, and that of the highest intuitive being which takes up all the rest of the nature into unity with the Divine. Practically, however, the others may be regarded as preparatory movements. For the Gita itself here says that it is only at the end of many existences that one can, after possession of the integral knowledge and after working that out in oneself through many lives, attain at the long last to the Transcendent. For the knowledge of the Divine as all things that are is difficult to attain and rare on earth is the great soul, *mahātmā*, who is capable of fully so seeing him and of entering into him with his whole being, in every way of his nature, by the wide power of this all-embracing knowledge, *sarvavit sarvabhāvena*.

It may be asked how is that devotion high and noble, *udāra*, which seeks God only for the worldly boons he can give or as a refuge in sorrow and suffering, and not the Divine for its own sake? Do not egoism, weakness, desire reign in such an adoration and does it not belong to the lower nature? Moreover, where there is not knowledge, the devotee does not approach the Divine in his integral all-embracing truth, *vāsudevaḥ sarvam iti*, but constructs imperfect names and images of the Godhead which are only reflections of his own need, temperament and nature, and he worships them to help or appease his natural longings. He constructs for the Godhead the name and form of Indra or Agni, of Vishnu or Shiva, of a divinised Christ or Buddha, or else some composite of natural qualities, an indulgent God of love and mercy, or a severe God of righteousness and justice, or an awe-inspiring God of wrath and terror and flaming punishments, or some amalgam of any of these, and to that he raises his altars without and in his heart and mind and falls down before it to demand from it worldly good and joy or healing of his wounds or a sectarian sanction for an erring, dogmatic, intellectual, intolerant knowledge. All this up to a certain point is true enough. Very rare is the great soul who knows that Vasudeva the omnipresent Being is all that is, *vāsudevaḥ sarvam iti sa mahātmā sudurlabhaḥ*. Men are led away by various outer desires which take from them the working of the inner knowledge, *kāmais tais tair hrtajñānāḥ*. Ignorant, they resort to other godheads, imperfect forms of the deity which correspond to their desire, *prapadyante'nyadevatāḥ*. Limited, they set up this or that rule and cult, tam tam *niyamam āsthāya*, which satisfies the need of their nature. And in all this it is a compelling personal determination, it is this narrow need of their own nature that they follow and take for the highest truth,—incapable yet of the infinite and its largeness. The Godhead in these forms gives them their desires if their faith is whole; but these fruits and gratifications are temporary and it is a petty intelligence and unformed reason which makes the pursuit of them its principle of religion and life. And so far as there is a spiritual attainment by this way, it is only to the gods; it is only the Divine in formations of mutable nature and as the giver of her results that they realise. But those who adore the transcendent and integral Godhead, embrace all this and transform it all, exalt the gods to their highest, Nature to her summits, and go beyond them to the very Godhead, realise and attain to the Transcendent. *Devān deva-yajo yānti madbhaktā yānti mām api.*

Still the supreme Godhead does not at all reject these devotees because of their imperfect vision. For the Divine in his supreme transcendent being, unborn, immutable and superior to all these partial manifestations, cannot be easily known to any living creature. He is self-enveloped in this immense cloak of Maya, that Maya of his Yoga, by which he is one with the world and yet beyond it, immanent but hidden, seated in all hearts but not revealed to any and every being. Man in Nature thinks that these manifestations in Nature are all the Divine, when they are only his works and his powers and his veils. He knows all past and all present and future existences, but him none yet knoweth. If then after thus bewildering them with his workings in Nature, he were not to meet them in these at all, there would be no divine hope for man or for any soul in Maya. Therefore according to their nature, as they approach him, he accepts their bhakti and answers to it with the reply of divine love and compassion. These forms are after all a certain kind of manifestation through which the imperfect human intelligence can touch him, these desires are first means by which our souls turn towards him: nor is any devotion worthless or ineffective, whatever its limitations. It has the one grand necessity, faith. "Whatever form of me any devotee with faith desires to worship, I make that faith of his firm and undeviating." By the force of that faith in his cult and worship, he gets his desire and the spiritual realisation for which he is at the moment fitted. By seeking all his good from the Divine, he shall come in the end to seek in the Divine all his good. By depending for his joys on the Divine, he shall learn to fix in the Divine all his joy. By knowing the Divine in his forms and qualities, he shall come to know him as the All and the Transcendent who is the source of all things.

## Absolute Self-Surrender

This absolute self-giving, this one-minded surrender is the devotion which the Gita makes the crown of its synthesis. All action and effort are by this devotion turned into an offering to the supreme and universal Godhead. "Whatever thou doest, whatever thou enjoyest, whatever thou sacrificest, whatever thou givest, whatever energy of tapasya, of the soul's will or effort thou puttest forth, make it an offering unto Me." Here the least, the slightest circumstance of life, the most insignificant gift out of oneself or what one has, the smallest action assumes a divine significance, and it becomes an acceptable offering to the Godhead who makes it a means for his possession of the soul and life of the God-lover. The distinctions made by desire and ego then disappear. As there is no straining after the good result of one's action, no shunning of unhappy result, but all action and result are given up to the Supreme to whom all work and fruit in the world belong for ever, there is no farther bondage. For by an absolute self-giving, all egoistic desire disappears from the heart and there is a perfect union between the Divine and the individual soul through an inner renunciation of its separate living. All will, all action, all result become that of the Godhead, work divinely through the purified and illumined nature and no longer belong to the limited personal ego. The finite nature thus surrendered becomes a free channel of the Infinite; the soul in its spiritual being, uplifted out of the ignorance and the limitation, returns to its oneness with the Eternal. The Divine Eternal is the inhabitant in all existences; he is equal in all and the equal friend, father, mother, creator, lover, supporter of all creatures. He is the enemy of none and he is the partial lover of none; none has he cast out, none has he eternally condemned, none has he favoured by any despotism of arbitrary caprice: all at last equally come to him through their circlings in the ignorance. But it is only this perfect adoration that can make this indwelling of God in man and man in God a conscious thing and an engrossing and perfect union. Love of the Highest and a total self-surrender are the direct and swift way to this divine oneness.

# The Eternal Promise of the Divine

The equal Divine Presence in all of us makes no other preliminary condition, if once this integral self-giving has been made in faith and in sincerity and with a fundamental completeness. All have access to this gate, all can enter into this temple: our mundane distinctions disappear in the mansion of the All-lover. There the virtuous man is not preferred, nor the sinner shut out from the Presence; together by this road the Brahmin pure of life and exact in observance of the law and the outcaste born from a womb of sin and sorrow and rejected of men can travel and find an equal and open access to the supreme liberation and the highest dwelling in the Eternal. Man and woman find their equal right before God; for the divine Spirit is no respecter of persons or of social distinctions and restrictions: all can go straight to him without intermediary or shackling condition. "If" says the divine Teacher, "even a man of very evil conduct turns to me with a sole and entire love, he must be regarded as a saint, for the settled will of endeavour in him is a right and complete will. Swiftly he becomes a soul of righteousness and obtains eternal peace." In other words a will of entire self-giving opens wide all the gates of the spirit and brings in response an entire descent and self-giving of the Godhead to the human being, and that at once reshapes and assimilates everything in us to the law of the divine existence by a rapid transformation of the lower into the spiritual nature. The will of self-giving forces away by its power the veil between God and man; it annuls every error and annihilates every obstacle. Those who aspire in their human strength by effort of knowledge or effort of virtue or effort of laborious self-discipline, grow with much anxious difficulty towards the Eternal; but when the soul gives up its ego and its works to the Divine, God himself comes to us and takes up our burden. To the ignorant he brings the light of the divine knowledge, to the feeble the power of the divine will, to the sinner the liberation of the divine purity, to the suffering the infinite spiritual joy and Ananda. Their weakness and the stumblings of their human strength make no difference. "This is my word of promise," cries the voice of the Godhead to Arjuna, "that he who loves me shall not perish." Previous effort and preparation, the purity and the holiness of the Brahmin, the enlightened strength of the king-sage great in works and knowledge have their value, because they make it easier for the imperfect human creature to arrive at this wide vision and self-surrender; but even without this preparation, all who take refuge in the divine Lover of man, the Vaishya once preoccupied with the narrowness of wealth-getting and the labour of production, the Shudra hampered by a thousand hard restrictions, woman shut in and stunted in her growth by the narrow circle society has drawn around her self-expansion, those too, *pāpa-yonayaḥ*, on whom their past Karma has imposed even the very worst of births, the outcaste, the Pariah, the Chandala, find at once the gates of God opening before them. In the spiritual life all the external distinctions of which men make so much because they appeal with an oppressive force to the outward mind, cease before the equality of the divine Light and the wide omnipotence of an impartial Power.

The earthly world preoccupied with the dualities and bound to the immediate transient relations of the hour and the moment is for man, so long as he dwells here attached to these things, and while he accepts the law they impose on him for the law of his life, a world of struggle, suffering and sorrow. The way to liberation is to turn from the outward to the inward, from the appearance created by the material life which lays its burden on the mind and imprisons it in the grooves of life and the body to the divine Reality which waits to manifest itself through the freedom of the spirit. Love of the world, the mask, must change into the love of God, the Truth. Once this secret and inner Godhead is known and is embraced, the whole being and whole life will undergo a sovereign uplifting and a marvellous transmutation. In place of the ignorance of the lower Nature absorbed in its outward works and appearances, the eye will open to the vision of God everywhere, to the unity and universality of the spirit. The world's sorrow and pain will disappear in the bliss of the All-blissful; our weakness and error and sin will be changed into the all-embracing and all-transforming strength, truth and purity of the Eternal. To make the mind one with the divine consciousness, to make the whole of our emotional nature one love of God everywhere, to make all our works one sacrifice to the Lord of the worlds and all our worship and aspiration one adoration of him and self-surrender, to direct the whole self Godwards in an entire union is the way to rise out of a mundane into a divine existence. This is the Gita's teaching of divine love and devotion, in which knowledge, works and the heart's longing become one in a supreme unification, a merging of all their divergences, an intertwining of all their threads, a high fusion, a wide identifying movement.

# THE MESSAGE OF THE GITA

What then is the message of the Gita and what its working value, its spiritual utility to the human mind of the present day following the long ages that have elapsed since it was written and the great subsequent transformations of thought and experience? The human mind moves always forward, alters its viewpoint and enlarges its thought substance, and the effect of these changes is to render past systems of thinking obsolete or, when they are preserved, to extend, to modify and subtly or visibly to alter their value. The vitality of an ancient doctrine consists in the extent to which it naturally lends itself to such a treatment; for that means that whatever may have been the limitations or the obsolescences of the form of its thought, the truth of substance, the truth of living vision and experience on which its system was built is still sound and retains a permanent validity and significance. The Gita is a book that has worn extraordinarily well and it is almost as fresh and still in its real substance quite as new, because always renewable in experience, as when it first appeared in or was written into the frame of the Mahabharata. It is still received in India as one of the great bodies of doctrine that most authoritatively govern religious thinking and its teaching acknowledged as of the highest value if not wholly accepted by almost all shades of religious belief and opinion. Its influence is not merely philosophic or academic but immediate and living, an influence both for thought and action, and its ideas are actually at work as a powerful shaping factor in the revival and renewal of a nation and a culture. It has even been said recently by a great voice that all we need of spiritual truth for the spiritual life is to be found in the Gita. It would be to encourage the superstition of the book to take too literally that utterance. The truth of the spirit is infinite and cannot be circumscribed in that manner. Still it may be said that most of the main clues are there, and that after all the later developments of spiritual experience and discovery we can still return to it for a immense inspiration and guidance. Outside India too it is universally acknowledged as one of the world's great scriptures, although in Europe its thought is better understood than its secret of spiritual practice. What is it then that gives this vitality to the thought and the truth of the Gita?

## Gita a Synthesis of Inner and Outer Life

The central interest of the Gita's philosophy and Yoga is its attempt, the idea with which it sets out, continues and closes, to reconcile and even effect a kind of unity between the inner spiritual truth in its most absolute and integral realisation and the outer actualities of man's life and action. A compromise between the two is common enough, but that can never be a final and satisfactory solution. An ethical rendering of spirituality is also common and has its value as a law of conduct; but that is a mental solution which does not amount to a complete practical reconciliation of the whole truth of spirit with the whole truth of life and it raises as many problems as it solves. One of these is indeed the starting-point of the Gita; it sets out with an ethical problem raised by a conflict in which we have on one side the dharma of the man of action, a prince and warrior and leader of men, the protagonist of a great crisis, of a struggle on the physical plane, the plane of actual life, between the powers of right and justice and the powers of wrong and injustice, the demand of the destiny of the race upon him that he shall resist and launch battle and establish even though through a terrible physical struggle and a massive slaughter a new era and reign of truth and right and justice, and on the other side, the ethical sense which condemns the means and the action as a sin, recoils from the price of individual suffering and social strife, unsettling and disturbed and regards abstention from violence and battle as the only way and the one right moral attitude. A spiritualised ethics insists on Ahinsa, on non-injuring and non-killing as the highest law of spiritual conduct. The battle, if it is to be fought out at all, must be fought on the spiritual plane and by some kind of non-resistance or refusal of participation or only by soul resistance, and if this does not succeed on the external plane, if the force of injustice conquers, the individual will still have preserved his virtue and vindicated by his example the highest ideal. On the other hand, a more insistent extreme of the inner spiritual direction, passing beyond this struggle between social duty and an absolutist ethical ideal, is apt to take the ascetic turn and to point away from life and all its aims and standards of action towards another and celestial or supracosmic state in which alone beyond the perplexed vanity and illusion of man's birth and life and death, there can be a pure spiritual existence. The Gita rejects none of these in their place,—for it insists on the performance of social duty, the following of the dharma for the man who has to take his share in the common action, accepts Ahinsa as part of the highest spiritual-ethical ideal and recognises the ascetic renunciation as a way of spiritual salvation. And yet it goes boldly beyond all these conflicting positions;

greatly daring, it justifies all life to the spirit as a significant manifestation of the one Divine Being and asserts the compatibility of a complete human action and a complete spiritual life lived in union with the Infinite, consonant with the highest Self, expressive of the perfect Godhead.

## Cause of the Problem

All the problems of human life arise from the complexity of our existence, the obscurity of its essential principle and the secrecy of the inmost power that makes out its determinations and governs its purpose and its processes. If our existence were of one piece, solely material-vital or solely mental or solely spiritual, or even if the others were entirely or mainly involved in one of these or were quite latent in our subconscient or our superconscient parts, there would be nothing to perplex us; the material and vital law would be imperative or the mental would be clear to its own pure and unobstructed principle or the spiritual self-existent and self-sufficient to spirit. Animals are aware of no problems; a mental god in a world of pure mentality would admit none or would solve them all by the purity of a mental rule or the satisfaction of a rational harmony; a pure spirit would be above them and self-content in the infinite. But the existence of man is a triple web, a thing mysteriously physical-vital, mental and spiritual at once, and he knows not what the true relations of these things are, the real reality of his life and his nature, whither the attraction of his destiny and where the sphere of his perfection.

Matter and life are his actual basis, the thing from which he starts and on which he stands and whose requirement and law he has to satisfy if he would exist at all on earth and in the body. The material and vital law is a rule of survival, of struggle, of desire and possession, of self-assertion and the satisfaction of the body, the life and the ego. All the intellectual reasoning in the world, all the ethical idealism and spiritual absolutism of which the higher faculties of man are capable cannot abolish the reality and claim of our vital and material base or prevent the race from following under the imperative compulsion of Nature its aims and the satisfaction of its necessities or from making its important problems a great and legitimate part of human destiny and human interest and endeavour. And the intelligence of man even, failing to find any sustenance in spiritual or ideal solutions that solve everything else but the pressing problems of our actual human life, often turns away from them to an exclusive acceptance of the vital and material existence and the reasoned or instinctive pursuit of its utmost possible efficiency, well-being and organised satisfaction. A gospel of the will to live or the will to power or of a rationalised vital and material perfection becomes the recognised dharma of the human race, and all else is considered either a pretentious falsity or a quite subsidiary thing, a secondary issue of a minor and dependent consequence. Matter and life however in spite of their insistence and great importance are not all that man is, nor can he wholly accept mind as nothing but a servant of the life and body admitted to certain pure enjoyments of its own as a sort of reward for its service or regard it as no more than an extension and flower of the vital urge, an ideal luxury contingent upon the satisfaction of the material life. The mind much more intimately than the body and the life is the man, and the mind as it develops insists more and more on making the body and the life an instrument —an indispensable instrument and yet a considerable obstacle, otherwise there would be no problem—for its own characteristic satisfactions and self-realisation. The mind of man is not only vital and physical, but an intellectual, aesthetic, ethical, psychic, emotional and dynamic intelligence, and in the sphere of each of its tendencies its highest and strongest nature is to strain towards some absolute of them which the frame of life will not allow it to capture wholly and embody and make here entirely real. The mental absolute of our aspiration remains as a partly grasped shining or fiery ideal which the mind can make inwardly very present to itself, inwardly imperative on its effort, and can even effectuate partly, but not compel all the facts of life into its image. There is thus an absolute, a high imperative of intellectual truth and reason sought for by our intellectual being; there is an absolute, an imperative of right and conduct aimed at by the ethical conscience; there is an absolute, an imperative of love, sympathy, compassion, oneness yearned after by our emotional and psychic nature; there is an absolute, an imperative of delight and beauty quivered to by the aesthetic soul; there is an absolute, an imperative of inner self-mastery and control of life laboured after by the dynamic will; all these are there together and impinge upon the absolute, the imperative of possession and pleasure and safe embodied existence insisted on by the vital and physical mind. And the human intelligence, since it is not able to realise entirely any of these things, much less all of them together, erects in each sphere many standards and dharmas, standards of truth and reason, of right and conduct, of delight and beauty, of love, sympathy and oneness, of self-mastery and control, of self-preservation and possession and vital efficiency and pleasure, and tries to impose them on life.

The absolute shining ideals stand far above and beyond our capacity and rare individuals approximate to them as best they can: the mass follow or profess to follow some less magnificent norm, some established possible and relative standard. Human life as a whole undergoes the attraction and yet rejects the ideal. Life resists in the strength of some obscure infinite of its own and wears down or breaks down any established mental and moral order. And this must be either because the two are quite different and disparate though meeting and interacting principles or because mind has not the clue to the whole reality of life. The clue must be sought in something greater, an unknown something above the mentality and morality of the human creature.

*

The mind itself has the vague sense of some surpassing factor of this kind, and in the pursuit of its absolutes frequently strikes against it. It glimpses a state, a power, a presence that is near and within and inmost to it and yet immeasurably greater and singularly distant and above it; it has a vision of something more essential, more absolute than its own absolutes, intimate, infinite, one, and it is that which we call God, Self or Spirit. This then the mind attempts to know, enter, touch and seize wholly, to approach it or become it, to arrive at some kind of unity or lose itself in a complete identity with that mystery, *āścaryam*. The difficulty is that this spirit in its purity seems something yet farther than the mental absolutes from the actualities of life, something not translatable by mind into its own terms, much less into those of life and action. Therefore we have the intransigent absolutists of the spirit who reject the mental and condemn the material being and yearn after a pure spiritual existence happily purchased by the dissolution of all that we are in life and mind, a Nirvana. The rest of spiritual effort is for these fanatics of the Absolute a mental preparation or a compromise, a spiritualising of life and mind as much as possible. And because the difficulty most constantly insistent on man's mentality in practice is that presented by the claims of his vital being, by life and conduct and action, the direction taken by this preparatory endeavour consists mainly in a spiritualising of the ethical supported by the psychical mind—or rather it brings in the spiritual power and purity to aid these in enforcing their absolute claim and to impart a greater authority than life allows to the ethical ideal of right and truth of conduct or the psychic ideal of love and sympathy and oneness. These things are helped to some highest expression, given their broadest luminous basis by an assent of the reason and will to the underlying truth of the absolute oneness of the spirit and therefore the essential oneness of all living creatures. This kind of spirituality linked in some way to the demands of the normal mind of man, persuaded to the acceptance of useful social duty and current law of social conduct, popularised by cult and ceremony and image is the outward substance of the world's greater religions. These religions have their individual victories, call in some ray of a higher light, impose some shadow of a larger spiritual or semi-spiritual rule, but cannot effect a complete victory, end flatly in a compromise and in the act of compromise are defeated by life. Its problems remain and even recur in their fiercest forms—even such as this grim problem of Kurukshetra. The idealising intellect and ethical mind hope always to eliminate them, to discover some happy device born of their own aspiration and made effective by their own imperative insistence, which will annihilate this nether untoward aspect of life; but it endures and is not eliminated. The spiritualised intelligence on the other hand offers indeed by the voice of religion the promise of some victorious millennium hereafter, but meanwhile half convinced of terrestrial impotence, persuaded that the soul is a stranger and intruder upon earth, declares that after all not here in the life of the body or in the collective life of mortal man, but in some immortal Beyond lies the heaven or the Nirvana where alone is to be found the true spiritual existence.

It is here that the Gita intervenes with a restatement of the truth of the Spirit, of the Self, of God and of the world and Nature. It extends and remoulds the truth evolved by a later thought from the ancient Upanishads and ventures with assured steps on an endeavour to apply its solving power to the problem of life and action. The solution offered by the Gita does not disentangle all the problem as it offers itself to modern mankind; as stated here to a more ancient mentality, it does not meet the insistent pressure of the present mind of man for a collective advance, does not respond to its cry for a collective life that will at last embody a greater rational and ethical and if possible even a dynamic spiritual ideal. Its call is to the individual who has become capable of a complete spiritual existence; but for the rest of the race it prescribes only a gradual advance, to be wisely effected by following out faithfully with more and more of intelligence and moral purpose and with a final turn to spirituality the law of their nature. Its message touches the other smaller solutions but, even when it accepts them partly, it is to point them beyond themselves to a higher and more integral secret into which as yet only the few individuals have shown themselves fit to enter.

## The Gita's Message to the Vital Man

The Gita's message to the mind that follows after the vital and material life is that all life is indeed a manifestation of the universal Power in the individual, a derivation from the Self, a ray from the Divine, but actually it figures the Self and the Divine veiled in a disguising Maya, and to pursue the lower life for its own sake is to persist in a stumbling path and to enthrone our nature's obscure ignorance and not at all to find the true truth and complete law of existence. A gospel of the will to live, the will to power, of the satisfaction of desire, of the glorification of mere force and strength, of the worship of the ego and its vehement acquisitive self-will and tireless self-regarding intellect is the gospel of the Asura, and it can lead only to some gigantic ruin and perdition. The vital and material man must accept for his government a religious and social and ideal dharma by which, while satisfying desire and interest under right restrictions, he can train and subdue his lower personality and scrupulously attune it to a higher law both of the personal and the communal life.

## To the Ethical Man

The Gita's message to the mind occupied with the pursuit of intellectual, ethical and social standards, the mind that insists on salvation by the observance of established dharmas, the moral law, social duty and function or the solutions of the liberated intelligence, is that this is indeed a very necessary stage, the dharma has indeed to be observed and, rightly observed, can raise the stature of the spirit and prepare and serve the spiritual life, but still it is not the complete and last truth of existence. The soul of man has to go beyond to some more absolute dharma of man's spiritual and immortal nature. And this can only be done if we repress and get rid of the ignorant formulations of the lower mental elements and the falsehood of egoistic personality, impersonalise the action of the intelligence and will, live in the identity of the one self in all, break out of all ego-moulds into the impersonal spirit. The mind moves under the limiting compulsion of the triple lower nature, it erects its standards in obedience to the tamasic, rajasic or at highest the sattwic qualities; but the destiny of the soul is a divine perfection and liberation and that can only be based in the freedom of our highest self, can only be found by passing through its vast impersonality and universality beyond mind into the integral light of the immeasurable Godhead and supreme Infinite who is beyond all dharmas.

## To the Seekers of the Absolute

The Gita's message to those, absolutist seekers of the Infinite, who carry impersonality to an exclusive extreme, entertain an intolerant passion for the extinction of life and action and would have as the one ultimate aim and ideal an endeavour to cease from all individual being in the pure silence of the ineffable Spirit, is that this is indeed one path of journey and entry into the Infinite, but the most difficult, the ideal of inaction a dangerous thing to hold up by precept or example before the world, this way, though great, yet not the best way for man and this knowledge, though true, yet not the integral knowledge. The Supreme, the all-conscious Self, the Godhead, the Infinite is not solely a spiritual existence remote and ineffable; he is here in the universe at once hidden and expressed through man and the gods and through all beings and in all that is. And it is by finding him not only in some immutable silence, but in the world and its beings and in all self and in all Nature, it is by raising to an integral as well as to a highest union with him all the activities of the intelligence, the heart, the will, the life that man can solve at once his inner riddle of self and God and the outer problem of his active human existence. Made Godlike, God-becoming, he can enjoy the infinite breadth of a supreme spiritual consciousness that is reached through works no less than through love and knowledge. Immortal and free, he can continue his human action from that highest level and transmute it into a supreme and all-embracing divine activity,—that indeed is the ultimate crown and significance here of all works and living and sacrifice and the world's endeavour.

## The Highest Message

This highest message is first for those who have the strength to follow after it, the master men and women, the great spirits, the God-knowers, God-doers, God-lovers who can live in God and for God and do their work joyfully for him in the world, a divine work uplifted above the restless darkness of the human mind and the false limitations of the ego. At the same time, and here we get the gleam of a larger promise which we may even extend to the hope of a collective turn towards perfection,—for if there is hope for man, why should there not be hope for mankind?—the Gita declares that all can if they will, even to the lowest and sinfullest among men, enter into the path of this Yoga. And if there is a true self-surrender and an absolute unegoistic faith in the indwelling

Divinity, success is certain in this path. The decisive turn is needed; there must be an abiding belief in the Spirit, a sincere and insistent will to live in the Divine, to be in self one with him and in Nature—where too we are an eternal portion of his being—one with his greater spiritual Nature, God-possessed in all our members and Godlike.

# THE SUPREME SECRET

## The Final Word

After giving out all the laws, the dharmas, and the deepest essence of its Yoga, after saying that beyond all the first secrets revealed to the mind of man by the transforming light of spiritual knowledge, *guhyāt*, this is a still deeper more secret truth, *guhyataram*, the Gita suddenly declares that there is yet a supreme word that it has to speak, *paramam vacaḥ*, and a most secret truth of all, *sarvaguhyatamam*. This secret of secrets the Teacher will tell to Arjuna as his highest good because he is the chosen and beloved soul, *iṣṭa*. For evidently, as had already been declared by the Upanishad, it is only the rare soul chosen by the Spirit for the revelation of his very body, *tanum svām*, who can be admitted to this mystery, because he alone is near enough in heart and mind and life to the Godhead to respond truly to it in all his being and to make it a living practice. The last, the closing supreme word of the Gita expressing the highest mystery is spoken in two brief, direct and simple slokas, and these are left without farther comment or enlargement to sink into the mind and reveal their own fullness of meaning in the soul's experience. For it is alone this inner incessantly extending experience that can make evident the infinite deal of meaning with which are for ever pregnant these words in themselves apparently so slight and simple. And we feel, as they are being uttered, that it was this for which the soul of the disciple was being prepared all the time and the rest was only an enlightening and enabling discipline and doctrine. Thus runs this secret of secrets, the highest most direct message of the Ishwara. "Become my-minded, my lover and adorer, a sacrificer to me, bow thyself to me, to me thou shalt come, this is my pledge and promise to thee, for dear art thou to me. Abandon all dharmas and take refuge in me alone. I will deliver thee from all sin and evil, do not grieve."

*

The Gita throughout has been insisting on a great and well-built discipline of Yoga, a large and clearly traced philosophical system, on the Swabhava and the Swadharma, on the sattwic law of life as leading out of itself by a self-exceeding exaltation to a free spiritual dharma of immortal existence utterly wide in its spaces and high-lifted beyond the limitation of even this highest guna, on many rules and means and injunctions and conditions of perfection, and now suddenly it seems to break out of its own structure and says to the human soul, "Abandon all dharmas, give thyself to the Divine alone, to the supreme Godhead above and around and within thee: that is all that thou needest, that is the truest and greatest way, that is the real deliverance." The Master of the worlds in the form of the divine Charioteer and Teacher of Kurukshetra has revealed to man the magnificent realities of God and Self and Spirit and the nature of the complex world and the relation of man's mind and life and heart and senses to the Spirit, and the victorious means by which through his own spiritual self-discipline and effort he can rise out of mortality into immortality and out of his limited mental into his infinite spiritual existence. And now speaking as the Spirit and Godhead in man and in all things he says to him, "All this personal effort and self-discipline will not in the end be needed, all following and limitation of rule and dharma can at last be thrown away as hampering encumbrances if thou canst make a complete surrender to Me, depend alone on the Spirit and Godhead within thee and all things and trust to his sole guidance. Turn all thy mind to me and fill it with the thought of me and my presence. Turn all thy heart to me, make thy every action, whatever it be, a sacrifice and offering to me. That done, leave me to do my will with thy life and soul and action; do not be grieved or perplexed by my dealings with thy mind and heart and life and works or troubled because they do not seem to follow the laws and dharmas man imposes on himself to guide his limited will and intelligence. My ways are the ways of a perfect wisdom and power and love that knows all things and combines all its movements in view of a perfect eventual result; for it is refining and weaving together the many threads of an integral perfection. I am here with thee in thy chariot of battle revealed as the Master of Existence within and without thee and I repeat the absolute assurance, the infallible promise that I will lead thee to myself through and beyond all sorrow and evil. Whatever difficulties and perplexities arise, be sure of this that I am leading thee to a complete divine life in the universal and an immortal existence in the transcendent Spirit."

## The Secret of Secrets

And now there comes the supreme word and most secret thing of all, *guhyatamam*, that the Spirit and Godhead is an Infinite free from all dharmas and though he conducts the world according to fixed laws and leads man through his dharmas of ignorance and knowledge, sin and virtue, right and wrong, liking and disliking and indifference, pleasure and pain, joy and sorrow and the rejection of these opposites, through his physical and vital, intellectual, emotional, ethical and spiritual forms and rules and standards, yet the Spirit and Godhead transcends all these, and if we too can cast away all dependence on dharmas, surrender ourselves to this free and eternal Spirit and, taking care only to keep ourselves absolutely and exclusively open to him, trust to the light and power and delight of the Divine in us and, unafraid and ungrieving, accept only his guidance, then that is the truest, the greatest release and that brings the absolute and inevitable perfection of our self and nature. This is the way offered to the chosen of the Spirit,—to those only in whom he takes the greatest delight because they are nearest to him and most capable of oneness and of being even as he, freely consenting and concordant with Nature in her highest power and movement, universal in soul consciousness, transcendent in the spirit.

For a time comes in spiritual development when we become aware that all our efforts and actions are only our mental and vital reactions to the silent and secret insistence of a greater Presence in and around us. It is borne in upon us that all our Yoga, our aspiration and our endeavour are imperfect or narrow forms, because disfigured or at least limited by the mind's associations, demands, prejudgments, predilections, mistranslations or half translations of a vaster truth. Our ideas and experiences and efforts are mental images only of greatest things which would be done more perfectly, directly, freely, largely, more in harmony with the universal and eternal will by that Power itself in us if we could only put ourselves passively as instruments in the hands of a supreme and absolute strength and wisdom. That Power is not separate from us; it is our own self one with the self of all others and at the same time a transcendent Being and an immanent Person. Our existence, our action taken up into this greatest Existence would be no longer, as it seems to us now, individually our own in a mental separation. It would be the vast movement of an Infinity and an intimate ineffable Presence; it would be the constant spontaneity of formation and expression in us of this deep universal self and this transcendent Spirit. The Gita indicates that in order that that may wholly be, the surrender must be without reservations; our Yoga, our life, our state of inner being must be determined freely by this living Infinite, not predetermined by our mind's insistence on this or that dharma or any dharma. The divine Master of the Yoga, *yogeśvaraḥ kṛṣṇaḥ*, will then himself take up our Yoga and raise us to our utmost possible perfection, not the perfection of any external or mental standard or limiting rule, but vast and comprehensive, to the mind incalculable. It will be a perfection developed by an all-seeing Wisdom according to the whole truth, first indeed of our human swabhava, but afterwards of a greater thing into which it will open, a spirit and power illimitable, immortal, free and all-transmuting, the light and splendour of a divine and infinite nature.

All must be given as material of that transmutation. An omniscient consciousness will take up our knowledge and our ignorance, our truth and our error, cast away their forms of insufficiency, *sarva-dharmān parityajya*, and transform all into its infinite light. An almighty Power will take up our virtue and sin, our right and wrong, our strength and our weakness, cast away their tangled figures, *sarva-dharmān parityajya*, and transform all into its transcendent purity and universal good and infallible force. An ineffable Ananda will take up our petty joy and sorrow, our struggling pleasure and pain, cast away their discordances and imperfect rhythms, *sarva-dharmān parityajya*, and transform all into its transcendent and universal unimaginable delight. All that all the Yogas can do will be done and more; but it will be done in a greater seeing way, with a greater wisdom and truth than any human teacher, saint or sage can give us. The inner spiritual state to which this supreme Yoga will take us, will be above all that is here and yet comprehensive of all things in this and other worlds, but with a spiritual transformation of all, without limitation, without bondage, *sarva-dharmān parityajya*. The infinite existence, consciousness and delight of the Godhead in its calm silence and bright boundless activity will be there, will be its essential, fundamental, universal stuff, mould and character. And in that mould of infinity the Divine made manifest will overtly dwell, no longer concealed by his Yogamaya, and whenever and as he wills build in us whatever shapes of the Infinite, translucent forms of knowledge, thought, love, spiritual joy, power and action according to his self-fulfilling will and immortal pleasure. And there will be no binding effect on the free soul and the unaffected nature, no unescapable crystallising into this or that inferior formula. For all the action will be executed by the power of the Spirit in a divine freedom, *sarva-dharmān parityajya*. An unfallen abiding in the transcendent Spirit, *param dhāma*, will be the foundation and the assurance of this spiritual state. An intimate understanding oneness with universal being and all creatures, released from the evil and suffering of the separate mind but wisely regardful of true distinctions, will be the conditioning power. A constant delight, oneness and harmony of the eternal individual here with the Divine and all that he is will be the effect of this integral liberation. The baffling problems of our human existence of which Arjuna's difficulty stands as an acute example, are created by our separative personality in the Ignorance. This Yoga, because it puts the soul of man into its right relation with God and world-existence and makes our action God's, the knowledge and will shaping and moving it his and our life the harmony of a divine self-expression, is the way to their total disappearance.

*

The whole Yoga is revealed, the great word of the teaching is given, and Arjuna the chosen human soul is once more turned, no longer in his egoistic mind but in this greatest self-knowledge, to the divine action. The Vibhuti is ready for the divine life in the human, his conscious spirit for the works of the liberated soul, *muktasya karma*. Destroyed is the illusion of the mind; the soul's memory of its self and its truth concealed so long by the misleading shows and forms of our life has returned to it and become its normal consciousness: all doubt and perplexity gone, it can turn to the execution of the command and do faithfully whatever work for God and the world may be appointed and apportioned to it by the Master of our being, the Spirit and Godhead self-fulfilled in Time and universe.